WE'RE RIGHT,
THEY'RE WRONG

SIMON & SCHUSTER

NEW YORK   LONDON   TORONTO   SYDNEY   TOKYO   SINGAPORE

WE'RE RIGHT, THEY'RE WRONG

✹✹✹✹✹✹✹✹✹

A HANDBOOK FOR
SPIRITED PROGRESSIVES

JAMES CARVILLE

RANDOM HOUSE ⌂ NEW YORK

Library of Congress Cataloging-in-Publication Data is available.
ISBN 0-679-76978-1

Printed in the United States of America on acid-free paper
987654

To Lucille "Nippy" Carville
and
in memory of Sam Adler

ACKNOWLEDGMENTS

✿✿✿✿✿✿✿✿✿✿✿

I don't usually do this sort of thing. I have found that it is immensely better politics just to say, "Y'all know who you are," and be done with it. But this time around, I owe such a debt of gratitude to so many people that I can't let these folks go without a big thank-you.

First and foremost, I am grateful to Lowell Weiss. If I were the kind of person who put justice before ego, Lowell's name would be on the cover of this book with mine. The least I can do is tell you that Lowell was the best collaborator and friend a guy could ever hope for. He lived with Mary and me out at our farm in Virginia for days at a time, and we missed him dearly every time he fled to write and think in relative peace.

Dalit Toledano took time out from law school to lend her genius to this book. She is talented and tenacious, a dedicated Democrat and a special friend.

Linda Kulman brought her considerable warmth and creativity to this project. She spent a lot of time in Louisiana, where my friends and family found her as intelligent and engaging as I did. Her contribution was invaluable. Jon Orszag was our go-to guy when it came to economics. This kid is a shoo-in for greatness, not only because he's so damned smart but also because he's always got a huge smile on his face. Josh Distler is a gifted researcher who compiled all of our best material on the federal government. Peter

Knobler, who collaborated with me and Mary on *All's Fair,* provided support for the chapter on race. He is definitely one of my favorite liberals.

I owe much to my two editors, David Rosenthal (Random House) and Alice Mayhew (Simon & Schuster), who were always right when I was wrong. How a coon ass like me merits the time and patience of two such eminent editors is hard to figure.

Mark Weiner was the perfect sounding board; over the last several months he has listened patiently and provided sage advice during countless lunches. I also want to thank my sage counsel, Robert Barnett, as well as my two best friends, Gus Weill and Gus Weill, Jr.

There were so many other kind folks who took the time to help out. Many contributed ideas and research, some provided remedial help with the issues, and most were on the receiving end of my frantic phone calls: Henry Aaron, Paul Begala, Eric Berman and the entire SWAT team at the DNC, Rebecca Blank, Barry Bosworth, Alan Brinkley, Deb Cohan, Sheldon Danziger, Todd DeLorenzo, Sheri Donovan, David Ellwood, James Fallows, Nathan Folse, Barney Frank, Al Franken, Matt Freeman and the folks at People for the American Way, Geoff Garin, Stan Greenberg, Robert Greenstein, Paul Griffin, Peter Hart, Jenn Hathaway, Christine Heenan, Al Hunt, Larry Katz, Mickey Kaus, Donald Kettl, Alan Krueger, Paul Krugman, Nolan LeBlanc, Nick Lemann, Frank Levy, Jon Macks, Sara McLanahan, Camilla Montgomery, Mandy Mosier, Carl Nash, Peter Orszag, LaDonna Pavetti, Charlie Peters, Richard Reeves, Uwe Reinhardt, Richard Riley, Geoff Rodkey, Bella Rosenberg, Amy Seif, Jennifer Selling, Robert Shapiro, Laura Sherman, Mark Shields, Eric Sklar, Theda Skocpol, Gene Sperling, Jim Spurger, Marcus Stanley, Huey Stein, George Stephanopoulos, Joe Stiglitz, Peter Stuckey, Larry Summers, David Thelan, Joanne Toledano, Cyril Vetter, Barbara Dafoe Whitehead, and Barry Zuckerman.

And finally, to President and Mrs. Clinton, who in addition to giving the country so much, have given me so very much.

CONTENTS

✱ ✱ ✱ ✱ ✱ ✱

INTRODUCTION

❋ ❋ ❋ ❋ ❋ ❋ ❋ ❋

The first person ever to slap me on the ass was a federal employee. He was the army doctor at Fort Benning, Georgia, who brought me into this world. My daddy was serving there at Fort Benning as an infantry officer, so he and my momma were able to start me off with some fine federal health care.

You'd have to say that the federal government made a big impression on me early in life. I grew up in a town in southern Louisiana by the name of Carville, and that's no coincidence; the town got that name because my family provided the town with its most indispensable federal employee—its postmaster. Three generations of Carvilles served as postmaster, starting with my great-grandmother Octavia Duhon. Believe it or not, working for the federal government was a source of family pride.

You see, the federal government was not considered a bad thing when I was growing up. First of all, it kept my feet dry. Before I was born, the Mississippi River used to overflow its banks every spring and flood the whole town of Carville and many other towns like it. It was a Washington bureaucrat who got the idea that we could build a levee system to stop the flooding, and the federal taxpayers helped us do it. It was the heavy hand of government at work.

In my hometown, the federal government also cared for a group of people no one else was willing to care for—folks from all over the country who came down with Hansen's disease, a condition more commonly known as leprosy. Carville was world famous as the home to the Gillis W. Long Hansen's Disease Center, where doctors developed the multidrug treatment that now allows people with Hansen's to lead a near-normal life. Only the federal government had the resources and inclination to do that.

Washington bureaucrats also came up with the idea that black children should be able to go to school with white children. Integration was *the* searing issue when I was a kid. After the *Brown v. Board of Education* decision in 1954, people in Carville, which was 85 percent black, stopped talking about football and the weather. All they wanted to do was scream about race. Like most whites, I took segregation for granted and wished the blacks just didn't push so damn hard to change it.

But when I was sixteen years old I read *To Kill a Mockingbird,* and that novel changed everything. I got it from the lady who drove around in the overheated old bookmobile in my parish—another government program, I might add. I had asked the lady for something on football, but she handed me *To Kill a Mockingbird* instead. I couldn't put it down. I stuck it inside another book and read it under my desk during school. When I got to the last page, I closed it and said, "They're right and we're wrong." The issue was literally black and white, and we were absolutely, positively on the wrong side. I've never forgotten which side the federal government was on.

Federal and state governments helped me get an education and a start in life. They offered me all kinds of loans and the G.I. Bill so I could earn myself undergraduate and law degrees at Louisiana State University. They picked up my salary when I served as a corporal in the United States Marine Corps and again when I taught eighth-grade science at a tiny little public school for boys in South Vacherie, Louisiana.

Government did right by me. I'm the first one to admit that fact. No, let's back up for a minute. I don't just admit that fact—I savor it. I hold it up as an example of what government should be in the business of doing: providing opportunity. You will never catch me saying that I am a self-made man. I am not. My parents gave me their love, their example, and the benefit of their hard work. And the government gave me a big hand.

Unfortunately, for a lot of politicians, it just isn't convenient to give the government any credit for the things it does right. Here's one of my favorite examples: Ronald Reagan used to love to talk about a guy named Joseph Giordano. He was the surgeon who saved Reagan's life in 1981, after the President was shot in front of the Washington Hilton. Dr. Giordano was Reagan's perfect human-interest story. He was the son of a milkman and the grandson of poor immigrants from Italy. Thanks to his own hard work and that of his parents, Giordano got himself through college and medical school and went on to become a prominent surgeon at a great hospital and then to save a president's life. The American Dream in spades.

But, you see, Dr. Giordano wasn't too enamored of the way Reagan was telling his life story. He thought the President had left a few details out of the picture—like school loans and federal funding for his medical research. Here's what Dr. Giordano said about the matter in the *Los Angeles Times* under the headline "Facts for the President's Fable": "The government social programs enacted over the last fifty years—and so frequently criticized by this President and his Administration—have played a vital role in making this success possible. . . . In contrast to the President, who feels that government programs make people so dependent that they lose initiative, I feel that these programs have enabled people with little resources to reach their full potential."[1] The doc said it all.

By telling Dr. Giordano's story and my story, I don't want to give you the idea that this book is just about people who operate on presidents or about political operators who help them get elected. In the past couple of months, I have had the opportunity to get to know a woman named Sheri Donovan, who is an even better case for what good can come from good government. No one in her family had ever attended college before. Her daddy finished the first grade and went no further. She's a twenty-seven-year-old unwed mother of three who just got herself off Virginia's welfare rolls, graduated from Lord Fairfax Community College with a 3.8 grade point average, and is now going on to the University of Virginia—financed by a heavy helping of school loans and grants. The government didn't tell Sheri Donovan it would do her homework for her, it just told her it would lend a hand if she wanted to help herself.

The purpose of this book is to say that we were right when we made investments in the Donovans and Giordanos and Carvilles of the world and that it's wrong to let the Republicans snatch these investments away to pay for tax cuts for those who don't need our help. It's all about priorities. I know that dollars are tight and the country just isn't growing like it was when I was a kid. But that should be all the more reason to invest wisely. To my way of thinking, there is no wiser investment than opportunity, no better way to hold this country together than to make sure everybody has at least a chance to get ahead.

Over the past year, while I've been writing this book, I've talked to economists around the country, people like Rebecca Blank, Frank Levy, Larry Katz, Alan Krueger, and Joe Stiglitz—the kind of folks whose IQs top my SAT score. What they tell me is that the typical American is doing no better—and in many cases significantly worse—today than he or she was twenty years ago. There are no quick fixes. But most of these economists say that one good way to turn this situation around over the long term is to get serious about investing in the education of our workforce.

It's pretty clear that we can't work much harder in this country. We're working plenty hard as it is, with more and more people taking two and three jobs just to make ends meet. But if we have more education and skills, we can work smarter and produce more in less time. It's what economists mean when they talk about trying to increase our "productivity."

There is no question in my mind that the government can make sure everybody who wants more education can get it. I'm not talking about sending everybody to Harvard and Princeton. I'm talking about investing in people so they can go to community colleges like the one Sheri Donovan went to. I'm talking about helping people get more skills.

A few years ago, one of my many nephews was trying futilely to break his Uncle James's record for utter academic failure by busting out of college without a job. My momma, who is known to most of Louisiana as Miss Nippy, informed my nephew that there were only two acceptable activities for a human being between the ages of five and sixty-five: being in training for a job or having a job. My nephew was doing neither, and that was unacceptable.

What Miss Nippy's 5/65 philosophy says to me is this: Work and training for work are core values. They are the values that built this country.

You see, I believe with all my heart that outside of love and faith, the most sacred thing you can render in this world is your labor. It certainly isn't any of the government's business whom you love or whom you worship. But it sure as hell should be its business to make sure you get the help you need in order to render your labor. So from here on out, you're going to hear a lot of talk about what we need to do to promote work and training for work. And I'm going to start calling myself a 5/65 Democrat. And I'll be happy to share the term with any of you.

As I see it, the great divide in this world is between people who believe that education, training, work, and opportunity are the essential ingredients to building a stronger and more prosperous nation—5/65 Democrats—and people who don't. You know who

I'm talking about. It's the people who want to cut school loans and grants so they can cut capital-gains taxes for the rich. People who want to get rid of the minimum wage under the false pretense that it hurts the folks it's meant to help. People who want to throw people off welfare without helping them get the tools they need to go to work. People who want to slash the earned income tax credit and other programs that reward people for lifting themselves up through work. People who want to raise taxes on middle-class wages so that they can scrap—that's right, *scrap*—taxes on stock-market investments. People who don't mind a health-care system in which prison inmates get coverage but 43 million Americans on the outside can't. People who have sucked from the government's sugar tit all their lives and now want to make sure it runs dry for everyone else. It's them versus us. Ours is the morally superior position. We're right, they're wrong.

Now that I'm in a proper fighting mood, I want to be real clear on who this book is for. First of all, it's for 5/65 Democrats, especially those who have been beaten on repeatedly over the past two years by blowhards whose only achievement in life is their ability to tune the dial on their AM radios. It is for those of you who are looking for the facts to contradict all those myths and falsehoods put out by the Republicans. It is for people who have had to put up with nauseating, inaccurate lectures from selfish airheads about the way the country was founded and what the Constitution really means. It is for people who understand that survival of the fittest is not an organizing principle for a democratic nation. But most of all, it is for every citizen of this great nation who is willing to fight just as hard for ordinary Americans and the country as a whole as these right-wingers are fighting for special interests and themselves.

If you're with me, fasten your seat belts. This book is going to shake you up and jostle you around. You're going to feel like you're cruising off-road with me in my Jeep.

Be prepared to zip around real fast from place to place, subject to subject, right-wing myth to right-wing myth. Also watch out for sudden pit stops, in the form of little sidebars in the text—I like to call them lagniappes, which is a Cajun word for "a little extra"; it's what we used to call the thirteenth beignet or donut.

la·gniappe (lan yap′, lan′yap), *n.* **1.** *Chiefly Southern Louisiana and Southeast Texas.* something given with a purchase to a customer, by way of compliment or for good measure.   **2.** a gratuity or tip. Also, **la·gnappe′**. [< LaF < AmerSp *la ñapa* the addition, equiv. to *la* fem. definite article + *ñapa*, var. of *yapa* < Quechua]

You're never going to be quite sure what this crazy Cajun is going to do next. But here we go. It's about time we got our act in gear.

WE'RE RIGHT,
THEY'RE WRONG

CARVILLE'S RAPID-RESPONSE TEAM COMES TO YOUR BACKYARD BARBECUE

❀❀❀❀❀❀❀❀❀❀❀

PART 1: EVERY DEMOCRAT'S NIGHTMARE

Last night I had a dream.

One of my wife's friends was going to have a huge barbecue for the Fourth of July. Sure, it was going to be a chest-thumping, live-free-or-die kind of Republican affair, but I have to admit, it sounded great. This friend has a big farmhouse set in the most beautiful part of Virginia, with acres of fields for our dogs to run around in and lots of cows for them to bark at. And based on prior experience, I knew the food was going to be first-rate. I will admit it: Republican gatherings always have better food than Democratic ones. Only good thing about a Republican party is the food.

Wouldn't you know it—at the last minute Mary couldn't go. She had to run off and give a speech at a convention of truck-stop hairdressers or some such thing, and I was on my own.

I was pissed. I had wanted to go to that barbecue real bad, but there was no way in hell I was going all by myself. I know my limits. Some of my best friends are Republicans, but without Mary to run interference from time to time, an all-Republican affair can be brutal. I made plans to watch the Marine Corps band play.

When Mary heard I wasn't going, she was screaming mad. She thought I'd be offending her friends by not showing up, and she just wasn't going to let me off the hook. But I held my ground. I wasn't going, goddammit. It was as simple as that.

Unfortunately, Mary, like many women, is a master of the ultimatum. She told me I was going to that barbecue or else she was going to start calling me Serpenthead on her TV show every night. I caved.

When I got to the farmhouse, the gravel road out front was jampacked with cars—all of them nice, most of them foreign. Some of the bumper stickers I saw were truly frightening:

Guns Don't Kill People
Kids on Welfare Do

Kiss Me!
I Just Resigned from the U.S. Senate

Screw the Geezers
They Don't Vote for Us Anyway

Get Govt. out of Medicare and
Back in the Bedroom Where It Belongs!

Man, it was going to be a rough crowd.

I took my two dogs out of my truck, put them on leashes, and walked around the back of the house, where all the music and good smells were coming from.

I was right about the chow. It was everything you would expect from a right-wing barbecue. I grabbed myself a paper plate and started in. The first thing I saw was a big wooden bowl full of that real good potato salad, the kind with homemade mayonnaise and fresh dill. And, sure enough, there were steaming-hot ears of Silver Queen corn. Then I got myself some tasty-looking beef brisket— you know, like three or four slices—with some real good Vidalia onions and a sweet Texas-style barbecue sauce and, for good measure, a tenderloin of pork.

CARVILLE'S TOP FIVE
RIDICULOUS AND PATHETIC REPUBLICANS

1. **Representative Fred Heineman** (R-NC)

   You wondering what those Republican freshmen are like? You know, the ones full of piss and vinegar, ready to bring on the revolution? Let me introduce you to Fred Heineman, who represents the Fourth Congressional District of North Carolina. His annual income is round-about, oh, say, $180,000.* Not too bad, I think most folks would agree. But Fred's got a different view of it. He describes himself as lower middle class and goes on to say, "When I see someone who is making anywhere from $300,000 to $750,000 a year, that's upper middle class." No wonder this guy doesn't mind slashing student loans and raising Medicare premiums. But I wonder if the people in his district, where 50 percent of families earn less than $34,569,† feel as if this clown is doing a good job for them up there on Capitol Hill.

2. **Representative Newt Gingrich** (R-GA)

   While I know you're not surprised that he made my list, you may be surprised to hear just how far Newt Gingrich's blame-government philosophy will take him. Recently, he admitted that he seldom worships at the Baptist church to which he belongs. Why the poor attendance record? He blamed it on redistricting.‡ So, Georgia gets new political boundaries, and Newt can't make it to church anymore. Now, I personally know of no local ordinance, no state law, no resolution in these here United States that would prevent a man from attending church outside his congressional district. But I pray for Newt's soul that I'm wrong.

3. **Senator Rick Santorum** (R-PA)

   AmeriCorps is a program created by the President to give young people a chance to improve their communities and then get the help they need to go to college. Sen. Rick Santorum hates the program: "Somebody is going to do one year of community service picking up trash in a park and singing 'Kumbaya' around a campfire and you're going to give him the equivalent of the G.I. bill?"§ This guy is a poster-boy Republican; according to him, the government can do no right; the private sector can do no wrong. Interesting, then, that the guy has been a government employee, collecting government paychecks, almost all of his adult life. In a party where big-time hypocrites can become superstars, watch out for this guy. He's got a bright future.

4. Lamar Alexander

Remember when this guy was Secretary Lamar Alexander? That's right, he headed up the Department of Education for two years under President Bush. And the last time he proposed a budget for the department, for fiscal year 1993, he asked for a 10 percent increase (which just happens to be double what the Clinton administration asked for fiscal year 1994).[||] Now, as a Republican candidate for President, he says he'd get rid of the whole damn thing. The key to this extraordinary change of heart is right-wing venom for the federal government in general and this department in particular. Pathetic and perverse pandering.

5. Michael Huffington

In case you've forgotten, Michael Huffington is the West Coast oil company heir who unsuccessfully tried to buy himself a U.S. Senate seat with nearly $30 million of his own money. When Huffington was recently asked which school his children attend, the question was more than he could deal with. "Saint... Saint... ask my wife," he stuttered.[#]

---

* Keith Bradsher, "Inequalities in Income Are Reported Widening," New York Times, Oct. 29, 1995.

† Michael Barone, The Almanac of American Politics 1996 (Washington, DC: National Journal, 1995), p. 1000.

‡ Mike Allen, "Gingrich: U.S. Strayed in Its Faith; Stresses Founding Fathers' Ideas of God's Role," Richmond Times-Dispatch, Oct. 10, 1995.

§ Katherine Q. Seelye, "The 1994 Campaign: Pennsylvania Senator," New York Times, Oct. 20, 1994.

|| Jack Anderson and Michael Binstein, "The Reeducation of Lamar Alexander," Washington Post, July 31, 1995.

Leah Garchik, "My Children? What Children?" San Francisco Chronicle, Apr. 5, 1995.

My plate was full to brimming, and I went over to the keg and pulled some ice-cold beer into a frosty glass. I looked up, scanning quickly to see who was around, and then made a beeline for the corner of the yard, back by the fence, where there was an open picnic table and some privacy. I couldn't wait to dig in.

I was about halfway through my corn when things started getting nasty. The country tunes they had been playing suddenly turned into the theme music from *Jaws,* and I saw a horde of Republicans making their way over to my table, moving in for the kill.

These were no ordinary Republicans. Leading the way was the one and only Newt Gingrich, his plate barely able to contain the Flintstone-size portion of spare ribs he had loaded on there. Right behind him were Rush Limbaugh, William Bennett, Bill Kristol, Pat Buchanan, Phil Gramm, Pat Robertson, and about twenty other right-wingers hell-bent on chewing me up and spitting out my remains on the lawn. Mary, God bless her, had dropped my Christian ass right in the middle of the Roman Colosseum.

CARVILLE'S TOP FIVE POTATO SALAD TIPS

1. Make Your Own Mayonnaise

2. Don't Overcook Your Potatoes

3. Don't Overtoss

4. Add Fresh Herbs
      (I like dill in particular)

5. Limit Your Ingredients
      (It's potato salad; make sure you can taste the potato)

As soon as they got within striking distance of my picnic table, they all sneered at me and asked, in unison, "Mind if we join you, Jim?" (Republicans are the only people who call me Jim.)

My first instinct was to set my two dogs on them. But then my squishy, softhearted liberal side took over—and I remembered that my dogs are harmless little lap puppies—and I invited the right-wingers to sit down. There were so many of them that most had to park themselves on the grass.

I don't mind telling you that I was sweating big-time. You see, I knew what I was in for. I was about to be held accountable for every social and economic ill that has beset this country during the past twenty-five years. Every street thug, drug pusher, purse snatcher, and crack cocaine baby. Every scrap of waste, fraud, and abuse in government. Every tax increase. Every federal regulation. Every bureaucrat. I was a sitting duck.

They all started firing at once. I couldn't hear what anyone was saying. It was all one horrific shouting match—you know, sort of like a quiet moment on *The McLaughlin Group.*

The next thing I know, my whole body starts shaking uncontrollably and I'm writhing on the ground. What the hell's going on? I try to stumble to my feet and—

Wait! I'm lying in bed! And here's Mary. I guess she was just shaking me to snap me out of my nightmare.

It was all so frighteningly real!

It's no wonder I had a nightmare like that. We Democrats have been taking a beating from rabid Republicans every place we go, from barbecues to Super Bowl parties to the neighborhood bar. We've lost all our campaign instincts. When there's bad information flying around out there, we think it unseemly to swat it down.

But guess what, folks? That strategy ain't working. It's one of the reasons we have so few Democrats in office and so much bad information.

I don't know what the hell has gotten into us, but we Democrats are too eager to give ground. We're a bunch of well-meaning weenies. We whine and anguish in public. I don't know any Republicans who talk up their major proposals by saying things like, "Well, it's not that good. It's the best we could do under the circumstances." And when was the last time you heard a red-blooded Republican—or a blue-blooded one, for that matter—saying in the middle of a debate "Well, there's a lot of truth to that" or "You've got a point there"?

Democrats do these things all the time. I've had enough of it. Many of the points we concede to them should never be conceded.

It's time we got our campaign-mode rapid response up and running again. And that's what these next few sections are all about. Here's where we're going to take on their nastiest, hairiest, ugliest myths one by one. The goal is to give you most of the information you need to do your own myth swatting right there at your own backyard barbecue.

Now, I don't want to put words in other people's mouths in order to do this little exercise. I'm going to use real quotes from real right-wingers. These ain't just straw flies.

And here's a word about technique: Sometimes when a fly lights on your burger or your brisket, it takes just a quick flick of the hand to make the fly think better of the proposition and move on. Some flies are more stubborn. It's the same thing with nitwits. Say you're at that barbecue and you've got half a mouthful of potato salad and some right-winger is all over you. If you're lucky, you might be able to get him off your case with just a quick flick of rapid response. But if he's spewing a persistent lie or if he's just a persistent twit, it might take the debate equivalent of a devastating forehand smash with a flyswatter to shut him up.

That's why I'm going to give you two swatting procedures. The first is the quick shoo-'em-away response—I believe this is called the sound bite. The second is the full-force extended response, in which we'll crush the myth under a weight of logic, facts, and statistics.

A RECIPE FOR YOUR
BACKYARD BARBECUE

Pork Tenderloin
4–6 lbs. pork tenderloin

> *marinade ingredients:*
> Paul Prudhomme's Pork and Veal Seasoning.
> garlic powder
> coarse black pepper

1. Put the tenderloin in a baking dish lined with aluminum foil.
2. Generously sprinkle with seasoning, garlic powder, and black pepper, covering the tenderloin.
3. Marinate in icebox overnight.

> *sauce ingredients:*
> 2 sticks real butter
> 1 tablespoon fresh pressed garlic
> juice of 2 fresh lemons
> 2½ teaspoons Paul Prudhomme's Pork and Veal Seasoning

1. Lightly sauté all the sauce ingredients in medium saucepan.
2. Place tenderloin over high heat on gas grill, and sear for five minutes on each side.
3. Take off high heat and place tenderloin on other burner.
4. Turn heat down to low. With the lid closed, cook for 45 minutes to 1 hour on indirect heat, basting periodically with the sauce.
5. After time is up, cook tenderloin over high heat for an additional 10 minutes on each side, then place on the top rack of the grill (not directly over heat).
6. Grill for another 15 minutes on low heat, turning once, while continuing to baste.

All it takes is a couple minutes of practice at home in front of the mirror. I guarantee it will make your next barbecue a whole lot more pleasant.

PART 2: THE MORNING AFTER

Let's start off this backyard barbecue drill by dispensing with one of the most foolish and baseless collections of myths ever put out there: that the 1980s were a rosy chapter in the nation's history. This will be a good warm-up exercise.

The reason this one is so easy is that we're not talking about some abstract theory here. We can fully assess the results, because we've got a decade's worth of numbers to look at. The verdict? *The Reagan years were a god-awful disaster that we're not going to recover from anytime soon.*

We'll get into the details in a minute, but let me just give you a whiff of Reagan's failure here. He promised us that he would balance the federal budget by 1984. Not even close. By the time he rode off into the sunset, Reagan had racked up almost $2 trillion in debt.

Let's forget for a minute the fact that $2 trillion of deficit spending was what allowed Reagan to post economic growth. Let's just look at what a hole that debt put us in. If it weren't for all the interest we're paying on the debt he and his Vice President ran up—it's costing us some $180 billion in interest this year alone[1]—we'd be in the black right now. Let me state that another way: If we didn't have to deal with the Reagan-Bush debt, we wouldn't be arguing over how and when to balance the budget. *We'd already have a balanced budget!*

Reagan also promised us economic growth like we'd never seen before. But take a look at the books: We got slower growth in the 1980s than we had in the 1970s.[2]

He promised that his tax cuts on the rich would lead to unprecedented growth in our productivity and savings. Wrong.

Productivity growth was pathetically anemic, and our savings rate plummeted.[3]

The whole damn thing was pure alchemy.

It's not hard to figure out what went wrong. A handful of goof-balls convinced Reagan to experiment with an untested concept called supply-side economics. It was the economic equivalent of jumping off the roof with an umbrella for a parachute—only instead of a busted ass, we got a busted Treasury.

This you must understand: At the time, supply-side economics was ridiculed by almost every serious *conservative* economist in the country. In the early 1980s, the main organization of professional economists, the American Economic Association, had 18,000 members. No more than 12—and I mean that literally—thought supply-side was for real. The other 17,988 members knew supply-side could never do anything close to what the goofballs claimed it would do.

Press coverage gave Americans the idea that supply-side theories split the economics profession and started a great intellectual bat-tle.[4] What a joke! It was a dozen flat-earth cranks against the whole economics profession. It's a testament to the greatness and com-passion of this nation that we didn't take all twelve of those guys, line them up against a cold concrete wall, light their cigarettes, and shoot them.

None of this is meant to be a personal attack. I know most of the people who beat the drum for supply-side economics, and almost every one of them is a decent human being. Take Art Laffer, for example. He's the guy who scribbled out the infamous Laffer curve, the intellectual foundation of the supply-side case, on a cocktail napkin while eating a pizza at some restaurant in New York. Even though that turned out to be the most costly pizza in American history, Art's one hell of a nice guy.

In my view, the supply-siders are not much different from other people in America with foolish ideas. I mean, we all have bad ideas from time to time. Say you're at a bar or on the golf course or at the Moose Club. You might hear someone talking about the virtues of cutting off the hands of people who steal loaves of bread. Or you might hear someone say we should build a thirty-foot wall around our borders to keep foreigners out. As asinine as those ideas are, I don't get myself worked up over that kind of talk. It's acceptable barroom banter. Mercifully, most of this banter doesn't leave the bar, and it never sees the light of day.

The problem is, the supply-siders' nonsense made it out of the bar and found an audience with a certain former California governor on the national campaign trail. And when that governor landed himself in the Oval Office, he smiled and asked us all to gamble trillions of dollars to see if those napkin sketches made any sense. They didn't.

A powerful minority got richer. The rest sat there waiting for trickles of prosperity that never came, and that result was no accident. It was the game plan all along!

JOBS ODDS

It's not too surprising that the Wall Street types overwhelmingly support the Republican Party. Hell, everyone knows the Republicans are better for the economy.

Actually, they're not. Since World War II, job growth has *always* been better under Democratic Presidents than under Republican ones. In the last fifty years, there have been ten Presidents—five Democrats and five Republicans—and the Democrats place first, second, third, fourth, and fifth.

Dumb luck? I was curious about that myself. So I called a couple of mathematician friends. They say that the chance of that occurring randomly is 1 in 252, which just happens to be almost the exact odds of being dealt a straight in a game of five-card stud.

How do I know? Reagan's own director of the Office of Management and Budget, the supply-side evangelist who was responsible for implementing the theory, admitted as much. I'll refresh your memory. In one of the most embarrassing confessions of all time, OMB director David Stockman told *The Atlantic Monthly,* "I mean, Kemp-Roth [Reagan's 1981 tax cut] was always a Trojan horse to bring down the top rate. . . . It's kind of hard to sell 'trickle down.' So the supply-side formula was the only way to get a tax policy that was really 'trickle down.' Supply-side is 'trickle-down' theory."[5] In other words, supply-side economics was just a fancy term for putting more money in the hands of the rich.

In 1992, we thought we had finally put the Trojan horse of trickle-down economics out to pasture. So much for that. No, the Republicans in Congress won't be giving us huge deficits all over again. But today we hear the same rusty 1980s rhetoric about stimulating growth by cutting capital-gains taxes and by slashing through environmental, consumer, and workplace protection. And later we're going to take a look at another supply-side idea from the 1980s that's rearing its ugly head in Congress: the flat tax. I wish it were unnecessary to rehash old business from that frightening decade. But no such luck. It's déjà vu all over again.

Let's go to the 1980s myths. You'll recognize all of these pronouncements and most of the Republicans spewing them. Again, the goal here is to load you up with live ammo. Take notes in the margins if you like.

❁ **The U.S. economy in the 1980s was the most incredible job-creating machine the world has ever seen.**
—John Rutledge, former Reagan adviser, and Deborah Allen, president of the Claremont Economics Institute, February 29, 1988[6]

RAPID RESPONSE

Cut the crap, boys and girls. Facts are facts. Reagan's job numbers weren't even as good as Johnson's, Carter's, Kennedy's, or Nixon's. And Clinton's stomping all over Reagan, too.

EXTENDED VERSION

Let's go to the numbers:

PRESIDENT	JOB GROWTH PER YEAR
Johnson	3.8%
Carter	3.1
Clinton	2.4
Kennedy	2.3
Nixon	2.3
Reagan	2.1
Bush	0.6

Based on data from the Bureau of Labor Statistics, Current Employment Statistics survey.

If that doesn't take a little wind out of their sails, focus just for a minute on Presidents Carter and Reagan and their *private-sector* jobs: Under Carter, 2.3 million private-sector jobs were created per year; under Reagan, only 1.8 million private-sector jobs were created per year.[7] You see, Reagan's job numbers, as unimpressive as they were, got a big boost from all the public-sector jobs—i.e., jobs for government bureaucrats—he was creating. In fact, in his two terms the economy added 1.4 million government bureaucrats to the payrolls, including 183,000 *federal* bureaucrats. That was one strange way of lifting the heavy hand of government off our backs.[8] And by the way,

President Clinton has already cut more federal jobs than Reagan added.

❀ **The economy . . . was purring along until it was derailed by the [Bush] budget "deal" of 1990.**—Martin Anderson, former Reagan domestic policy adviser, now a senior fellow at Stanford's Hoover Institution, spring 1991, on Bush's agreement to raise taxes and reduce the deficit[9]

RAPID RESPONSE
A lot of stupid things are said in our nation of 260 million people during the course of a year. I defy anyone to come up with something more stupid than this. Bush signed his tax increase into law in November 1990. The recession hit *four months earlier*—in July 1990.

EXTENDED VERSION
This myth is a major pillar of the Reagan case. It is what shields Reagan and the supply-siders from all blame for the dismal recession that hit a year after they left office. The theory at work here—the one sketched out on that cocktail napkin—is that taxes are everything. When taxes are lowered, the economy goes through the roof. When taxes are raised, the economy goes to hell. Under this theory, taxes are such a powerful force that Bush could sink a $6 trillion economy *before* he signed his tax increase into law. You see, in their zeal to make Bush the fall guy for their own failed economic strategy, the supply-siders didn't even manage to come up with a believable lie. Seeing these guys pin all the blame on Bush almost makes you feel sorry for him. Almost.

❀ **The amazing thing about cutting taxes was that it increased revenues.**—William Safire, *New York Times* columnist, February 21, 1995[10]

RAPID RESPONSE

The idea that you can cut taxes and increase government revenues is the equivalent of those diet schemes where you eat a lot of French fries and chocolate ice cream and then you're supposed to lose weight. It would be real nice if it worked. It doesn't.

EXTENDED VERSION

Let me be real clear on this one. The supply-siders promised that tax cuts would pay for themselves—and then some—because they would give the economy such a shot in the arm. The truth is that Reagan's tax cuts never even came close to paying for themselves. If it wasn't obvious enough just from the size of the deficit they ran up, the Department of Commerce found that individual tax revenues fell short by tens of billions of dollars every single year after Reagan's tax cuts.[11] Benjamin Friedman, a Harvard University economics professor, sums up the case: "Tantalizing as it was, Reagan's claim that lower tax rates would enlarge tax revenues never had substance."[12]

✱ **The budget was essentially a deal between Ronald Reagan and Tip O'Neill. Tip would always want to do more spending and Reagan would always want to do more tax cutting. "OK, we'll let you cut some taxes, if you let me spend a little more money."**—William Safire, February 21, 1995[13]

RAPID RESPONSE

And look here. Another case where we can slam-dunk Safire. As much as Safire knows about words, he doesn't have a clue when it comes to arithmetic. The truth of the matter is that Ronald Reagan requested more spending from Congress than Tip O'Neill authorized.[14]

EXTENDED VERSION

If Congress had rubber-stamped every single Reagan budget, the debt would be higher—by $29.4 billion—not lower.[15] Reagan was so keen on defense that he wanted to outspend O'Neill. I've got to hand it to Reagan: You've hit the big time when you want to outspend Tip O'Neill.

And don't you forget either that one house of Congress wasn't even under Democratic control when the debt first went through the roof. Republicans ran the Senate from 1981 to 1987, with Bob Dole in charge of the Senate Finance Committee before he became Majority Leader.

The reason they had to come up with the blame-Tip myth is, as I said before, the supply-siders had promised that their formula for growth would actually wipe out the big deficits they were running up. When that didn't happen, they had to blame somebody. God forbid they admit that they themselves broke the bank.

At least some Republicans are honest about it. Once again, my friends, Reagan's budget director David Stockman:

The root problem goes back to the July 1981 frenzy of excessive and imprudent tax cutting that shattered the nation's fiscal stability. A noisy faction of Republicans have willfully denied this giant mistake of fiscal governance and their own culpability in it ever since. Instead, they have incessantly poisoned the political debate with a mindless stream of anti-tax venom, while pretending that economic growth and spending cuts alone could cure the deficit.[16]

A devastating body blow if I've ever seen one.

✱ **In the early 1980s we set out to create conditions that would expand the U.S. economy. We passed tax cuts across the board for every taxpayer.**—Ronald Reagan, July 8, 1993[17]

RAPID RESPONSE

Sorry to rain on your parade, but at least 40 percent of American taxpayers had a bigger bite taken out of their paychecks at the end of the 1980s than they did when Reagan took office.[18]

EXTENDED VERSION

While Reagan was giving with one hand, he was taking with the other. Personal taxes went down, but Social Security, Medicare, and other taxes went up. The take-away part wasn't much of a problem for the rich, whose personal tax cuts were large and whose Medicare and Social Security taxes were capped. The overall tax load on the top 1 percent decreased from 32 percent in 1980 to 26 percent in 1990.[19] During the same period, the tax load on the bottom 40 percent actually increased.

✸ **The new policies and mind-set unleashed . . . a dynamic outburst of entrepreneurial creativity.**
—Robert L. Bartley, editorial page editor of *The Wall Street Journal*, 1992[20]

RAPID RESPONSE

I'd say it unleashed a five-year orgy of junk bonds, junk takeovers, and junk economics.

EXTENDED VERSION

You don't have to take my word for it. Let's hear from Richard Darman, one of the most prominent Republicans in Washington. In the aftermath of the S&L crisis, Darman said, "Some of our most creative and energetic private sector talents are motivated to invent paper transactions that merely reward financial manipulators rather than expand private productive capacity. And in the world of fast-moving deals, institutions responsible for longer-term investment feel obligated to chase near-term financial plays."[21] In plain English, Wall Street clobbered Main Street.

❁ **Ronald Reagan "is the man to whom we Americans owe a debt that we will never be able to repay."**—Rush Limbaugh, 1992[22]

RAPID RESPONSE
Amen, brother. Amen.

PART 3: WELFARE AS THEY KNOW IT

I'll let you know right up front that this go-round at the barbecue won't be quite as easy as the last. Why? Because there is nothing right-wingers love to talk about as much as welfare. It's got all three of the things that they obsess about most: money, race, and sex. It's a perfect hat trick.

Not to worry. You've done your homework. Their tired welfare myths are no match for the truth.

But I've got to hand it to the Republicans. It's simply masterful what they've done so far in this debate. They've managed to convince the American people that they have only two choices on welfare:

1. *Spend less money and cure all of society's problems*
     or
2. *Spend more money and make the problems worse*

What a coup! Before they hit on this logic, right-wingers actually had to admit that they didn't like paying to help poor people. And even right-wingers didn't feel real good about fessing up to that. It looked unseemly, to say the least. One of the GOP's finest, Rep. Sonny Bono, has given us a particularly vivid example of this kind of unseemliness: "Nobody handed me anything. I don't think I have to share it with anyone. I did it, and it's mine."[23] In my humble opinion, Sonny wouldn't have amounted to much of anything if he had never met Cher, but that's beside the point. The point is that naked greed looks ugly.

Now, thanks to the Republicans' fine maneuver, people have a much more respectable option: They can claim it's not greed. It's compassion. Hell, they care too much about people to give them a hand!

There's just one problem: The Republicans' message is based on nothing but wishful thinking. Yes, we have huge problems of dependency and out-of-wedlock births in this country, but welfare spending did not create these problems. And cutting welfare isn't going to cure them.

The economy has rejected most welfare recipients—not the other way around. Sure, the fear of getting thrown out into the streets will give a few people the kick in the pants they need. But our high-tech economy just isn't producing a whole lot of jobs for welfare recipients. After a point, you can kick people until your foot gets sore and it isn't going to do any good. As I'm sure I don't need to remind you folks, most welfare recipients don't exactly have an abundance of skills or education to back them up.

It doesn't feel too good to say this, but the only way to help these folks is to spend more money, not less. As much as right-wingers complain about the money we're already spending, the current system is cheap. The system I'd like to see is one that recognizes that spending a dollar and a half on getting someone into the workforce is far superior to spending a dollar on a handout. You see, if we actually cared about reforming welfare, we'd have to make work pay, and that adds up:

• We'd have to help more people with child care.
• We'd have to increase the minimum wage. If it doesn't rise this year, the purchasing power of the minimum wage will sink to the lowest it's been since 1955.[24]

• We'd have to figure out which of our job-training and education programs work best and then pay to make them available to every person who wants new skills. People would much rather earn a paycheck than pick up a welfare check.

• We'd have to end the absurd system of giving health insurance to people on welfare and not making it widely available to the working poor. In fact, if you asked some welfare experts what would be the single best way of helping people off the welfare rolls, the answer would come back real fast: universal health care. Some would go so far as to say that a quarter of the 5 million families on welfare would drop off the rolls tomorrow if we had the good sense to come up with some way of including everyone in the health-care system.[25]

• We'd have to keep the tax burden low on folks working their way out of poverty. We have a good program to do that. It's called the earned income tax credit. It's been around since the Ford administration, and Ronald Reagan, of all people, called it "the best antipoverty, the best profamily, the best job-creation measure to come out of Congress."[26] Now Republicans in Congress want to slash it.

The bottom line is that, if we're serious about reform, we've got to help people climb up the first rung of the economic ladder to get them toward independence. And we've got to make that first rung look more appealing. If I were a welfare recipient, I don't know that I'd be much interested in climbing up onto that rickety first rung the way things are now. With a pathetically lousy minimum wage, no health care, and no day care, welfare makes a lot more sense than many jobs. We've got to change the incentives. If you work, you should not be poor!

The most depressing part of this welfare debate is that the Republicans used to talk some sense. They used to talk about attacking welfare dependence by lifting people out of welfare instead of just throwing them off it. They almost sounded like 5/65 Democrats.

But then a funny thing happened. The Republicans decided that work wasn't that important after all. In fact, Charles Murray, coauthor of *The Bell Curve,* the unreadable right-wing bible on race and intelligence, began telling people that "getting women to work is not my definition of success."[27]

Whoa! They pulled a complete 180. And how did they explain their change of heart? Of course they were not about to admit to the American people that it was all a question of money and tax cuts for the wealthy. Well, Murray gave them an out. He told them that the real problem wasn't work. It was illegitimacy. Getting welfare mothers into work wasn't going to do a thing to stop them from having kids out of wedlock, so why bother putting money into making work more attractive?

You don't have to sell us 5/65 Democrats on the idea that daddies matter. Out-of-wedlock births *are* a huge problem in this country. Kids are better off with two parents. It's like catching a ball—two hands are better than one. Of course, every once in a while, someone makes a brilliant one-handed snag, and there are some kids who do fine with one parent. But in general you're better off sticking to two. Every statistic I've read makes that point in spades.

But what causes illegitimacy? After exhaustive study, we have finally found the answer that has eluded so many people: Illegitimacy is the result of unprotected copulation between post-pubescent males and females who are not married to each other.

Does the heavy hand of government, you ask, have a role in all this? Not much, if any. If you read any of the research, it's impossible to argue that welfare is a significant cause of the rise in single-parent families.

Let's use our own common sense:

• Since 1972, the value of the average monthly Aid to Families with Dependent Children check has withered away by 40 percent.

If you throw in food stamps, too, the benefit has fallen 26 percent. But the ratio of out-of-wedlock births has risen in the same period by 140 percent.[28] If welfare caused women to have kids out of wedlock, wouldn't you expect out-of-wedlock births to fall as the welfare benefits shrank?

• States that have lower welfare benefits usually have more out-of-wedlock births than states with higher benefits. If welfare caused out-of-wedlock births, wouldn't you expect the reverse?

• The teen out-of-wedlock-birth rate in the United States is off the charts compared with the rate in countries where welfare benefits are downright generous. If welfare caused out-of-wedlock births, wouldn't you expect countries offering higher benefits to have higher rates of out-of-wedlock births?

So if it wasn't welfare, like the Republicans claim, what caused this mess? Part of it has to do with changing values throughout society. A much larger cause is the changing nature of our economy.

The character of this nation fundamentally shifted right around 1973. Up until that time, we had poverty on the ropes; from 1960 to 1973, we cut the poverty rate in half.[29] Lots of folks were saying that there would be no more poverty by the turn of the century.

But in 1973 the bottom fell out of the economy, and poverty started rising again. The poverty rate in the United States became and has remained the highest in the industrialized world. In Harlem fourteen people now fight for every $4.25-an-hour fast-food job. Wages for all but the best educated are, as Peter Kilborn of *The New York Times* put it, "the stingiest since President Franklin D. Roosevelt created the welfare system."[30]

Unfortunately, people don't want to hear about long-term changes in the global economy when they're looking for answers to the problems of crime and out-of-wedlock birth and poverty. They want something easier. And the Republicans came up with the perfect solution: "It's welfare, stupid." Now they've gone one step further: They say the more we cut, the better off we'll be.

This is bullshit. The divide on welfare is very clear. Right-wingers believe that welfare reform is about cutting costs and adding punishment. Five/65 Democrats believe it's about teaching people the value of work and independence. You know the proverb about feeding people? Give a man a fish and he'll eat for a day. Teach him how to fish and he'll eat for a lifetime. We believe in giving people fishing lessons and even cooking up a fillet or two for them while they're learning. The Republicans no longer believe in fishing lessons. All they want to do is drain the pond.

And now, it's time to do a little rapid-response:

❈ **Since the onset of the War on Poverty, the United States has spent over $5.3 trillion on welfare. But during the same period, the official poverty rate has remained virtually unchanged.**—Robert Rector, Heritage Foundation, August 9, 1994[31]

RAPID RESPONSE
The answer to this is simple: (a) not in our wildest dreams have we spent that much, and (b) we don't do nearly enough.

EXTENDED VERSION
Usually, Republicans like us to believe that the people who get "welfare" are all single black mothers in the inner cities. But when they want to make the case that our country has spent an obscene quantity of money on "welfare," suddenly their definition grows. It includes middle-income students attending college with government-backed loans. It includes Grandma in the nursing home. And, in the cruelest irony of all, it includes families who get tax credits for working and staying off the dole. In fact, it includes everyone who's ever

qualified for a cent of the government's cash or an ounce of its care based on his or her income.

The other part of this quote that burns me is the idea that it doesn't do a lick of good to put money into social programs. That's ridiculous. First of all, the poverty rate today is *20 percent lower* than when we kicked off the War on Poverty, and *we've cut the rate of elderly poverty in half.* And second, if it weren't for these benefits, the poverty rate would be much higher. You'd see breadlines as long as in the Depression.

Want to know why we've still got too many poor people? It's not because our programs are inefficient. It's because we don't do enough. The slump in our economy since 1973 has been kicking the heck out of people without skills, and we as a country aren't losing any sleep over that fact. We have the thinnest, most pathetic social safety net of any industrialized country. And—surprise, surprise—we have by far the highest poverty level.[32]

❋ **The social safety net that we erected . . . has become a hammock.**—Sen. Phil Gramm (R-TX), May 5, 1995[33]

RAPID RESPONSE
Phil Gramm should know about government hammocks. With the possible exception of money he got from his investments in porn flicks, the man has been living off government paychecks his whole adult life.

EXTENDED VERSION
Our safety net is not a hammock but a ratty piece of cheesecloth.

Here are the facts: The average AFDC and food stamp benefits have gone down by more than a quarter over the past two decades. Right now, for a family of three, they don't even add up to $8,000 a year.[34] No one is lying in the shade, sipping rum punch, on that.

❁ **Let's reform welfare and demand that able-bodied men and women riding in the wagon on welfare get out of the wagon and help the rest of us pull.**—Sen. Phil Gramm, May 5, 1995[35]

RAPID RESPONSE
What a joke! The Republicans don't want these people to help pull the wagon. All they care about is tossing them and their kids off it. They're not stupid: Everyone in politics knows

---

PHIL GRAMM: WARD OF THE STATE

Phil Gramm is the quintessential hypocrite when it comes to government support. From the moment he was born, in a military hospital, he's been a first-class passenger on the wagon of government. The government paid for him to attend the Georgia Military Academy. It paid for him to get a degree at the University of Georgia. It paid for his graduate work. It paid him to be a consultant to the U.S. Bureau of Mines and the Department of Health, Education, and Welfare. It paid his honoraria when he gave commencement speeches at public universities. It paid his salary when he was teaching economics. It has paid his salary in Congress for seventeen years. As far as I can figure, the man has never held a private-sector job.

About a year ago, the staff at the NBC News show *Meet the Press* put together a list of all the ways Gramm had fed at the public trough. They estimated that in today's dollars, Phil Gramm has gotten $3.5 million in direct assistance from the taxpayers. If you throw in his government pension, it would top $4.6 million.

---

you can gain a few points by beating up on welfare mothers and immigrants.

EXTENDED VERSION
If the Republicans wanted more people to pull the wagon, they'd have to help people find work and training for work. But once the Republicans decided that they were going to balance the budget and cut taxes at the same time, work and training didn't look so appealing. Their answer was to drop the money for helping people find work and let the states do whatever the hell they wanted. It doesn't take a genius to figure out that the states have every incentive to start a "race to the bottom"; any state that offers extra job assistance or extra cash will attract unwanted poor people from other states.

❋ **We have got to stop giving people more and more money to have more and more children on welfare.**
—Sen. Phil Gramm, May 5, 1995[36]

RAPID RESPONSE
Sen. Pete Domenici (R-NM) had a mighty fine rapid response to this one. He said that if you believe cutting down on welfare benefits will cut down on births, "you believe in the tooth fairy."[37]

EXTENDED VERSION
Jim Florio, the former governor of New Jersey (and a close friend of mine), thought Gramm and people like him had a good point there. So he instituted a "family cap," which cut off benefits to women who have kids while they're already on welfare. Unfortunately, it looks like it isn't working. After two years, the rate of out-of-wedlock births has been about the same for those who got capped and those who didn't.[38] Looks like we'd have to conclude that these women weren't bringing kids into this world just to collect an extra $64 a month.

✸ **Welfare is a "system that fosters illegitimacy and its attendant social pathologies."**—William J. Bennett, former Secretary of Education and drug czar, February 1, 1994[39]

RAPID RESPONSE

I don't mind taking it on again. We shot this idea down early on in this section, but if welfare caused out-of-wedlock births, why would births go up as welfare payments go down? Why would states with the lowest payments generally have the most out-of-wedlock births? Why would countries with the highest payments have the lowest number of out-of-wedlock births? And why would a family cap have no effect on out-of-wedlock births?

EXTENDED VERSION

Here's what recent studies have concluded about the link between illegitimacy and welfare, courtesy of Tufts University's Center on Hunger, Poverty, and Nutrition Policy:[40]

A 1994 Urban Institute study found that
 • *"Among low-income single women who were themselves raised in single-parent families, size of welfare benefits has no significant influence on first births, subsequent births, or out-of-wedlock births."*[41]

A 1993 study from the University of Wisconsin found that
 • *"AFDC benefits have no influence at all on the decisions of Black women and only slight influence on never-married White and Hispanic women's decisions to have a first child."*
 • *"The possibility of receiving more benefits does not enter into the decisions women on welfare may make about having another child."*[42]

A 1994 study from the University of California at Berkeley's Graduate School of Public Policy found that
 • *"AFDC payments have no significant effect on decisions to have children among single mothers."*[43]

And by the way, Charles Murray himself studied the question and, to his great embarrassment, could find no direct link between out-of-wedlock births and welfare benefits among blacks.

✸ **We have developed a system that destroys families rather than saves them.**—Rep. Susan Molinari (R-NY), July 9, 1995[45]

✸ **We have funded a system that is cruel and destroys families.**—Rep. Newt Gingrich (R-GA), April 7, 1995[46]

✸ **Welfare . . . has created a whole culture of dependent people that is destroying the fabric of families.**—Rep. Tom DeLay (R-TX), June 2, 1994[47]

RAPID RESPONSE

Let me give you a dose of their logic here. If you've got a common cold and you take aspirin, your headache may go away but you may still feel pretty lousy. A reasonable person would conclude that aspirin isn't very good at getting rid of the underlying causes of the cold. Right-wingers, however, would conclude that aspirin caused the cold in the first place.

EXTENDED VERSION

I gave you three quotations here. I could have given you 3,000. There is hardly a Republican out there who has not said something like this in the past year.

Our current welfare system is no gem. It has bad incentives. But to say that it is the cause of family breakdown in this country is to completely ignore poverty. In the 1970s, the economy collapsed. The American family took it on the nose. Before the collapse of the economy, about 85 percent of young men working full-time were bringing home wages that could lift a family of four out of poverty. In 1994, it was only about 60 percent. In less than two decades, the wages of male high school dropouts have fallen by 25 percent.[48] Even male high school graduates are making 20 percent less in wages.[49] Let's face it—no one's lining up to marry guys who can't pay the bills.

✹ **Do not feed the alligators.**—on a placard held up by Rep. John L. Mica (R-FL) during debate on the House welfare bill, March 23, 1995[50]

RAPID RESPONSE
I don't know much about the guy who held up this sign, but I do know that he got a 100 percent approval ranking from the Christian Coalition. But has this guy even read the Bible? He's sure as heck not reading from any Bible I've ever seen.

EXTENDED VERSION
I suggest that anybody who thinks of our welfare children as alligators should take a look at a new study by economists Timothy Smeeding and Lee Rainwater.[51] They gave us a piece of good news: We don't have the poorest kids in the industrialized world. It turns out that our poor kids are only the *third* poorest!

And let's talk about the mothers and fathers who receive welfare. Are they greedy alligators or lazy bums? Of course not. When you ask welfare recipients themselves whether they should get something for nothing, 75 percent say no. These people have no difficulty with the idea that they should work for benefits.[52] So what's the problem? Two things: low skills, few jobs.

Don't take my word for it. I turn the floor over to Sheldon Danziger and Jeffrey Lehman, two eminent professors at the University of Michigan: "It is simply not the case that most of today's welfare recipients could obtain stable employment that

AMERICA'S POOR KIDS: NEAR ROCK BOTTOM

Here's a ranking of industrialized countries by living standards of poor children:

1. Switzerland	10. Austria
2. Sweden	11. Canada
3. Finland	12. France
4. Denmark	13. Italy
5. Belgium	14. United Kingdom
6. Norway	15. Australia
7. Luxembourg	**16. United States**
8. Germany	17. Israel
9. Netherlands	18. Ireland

Source: Lee Rainwater and Timothy Smeeding, *Doing Poorly: The Real Income of American Children in a Comparative Perspective*, Luxembourg Income Study Working Paper Number 127, Aug. 1995.

would lift them and their children out of poverty, if only they would try harder. Fear of destitution is a powerful incentive to survive; it will not, however, guarantee that an unskilled worker who actively seeks work will be able to earn enough to support her family."[53]

❀ **What has happened is you've had people elected to Congress who wanted to tell states and cities how to run their business and we've changed that and what we're going to try to do is to let local officials make local decisions.**—Sen. Phil Gramm, January 1, 1995[54]

RAPID RESPONSE

I'm all for state experimentation. Some states are already doing clever things. But punting to the states and the District of Columbia is not the answer to our welfare mess. It's just a way to tear down one welfare bureaucracy to build up fifty-one others, while scrapping all federal quality control and oversight.

EXTENDED VERSION

If you want support for the proposition that giving block grants to the states won't help the problem, listen to John DiIulio, a professor at Princeton who is an expert on public management. He told *U.S. News* that block grants "are a way of spending money the federal government doesn't have, for purposes that it won't specify, with consequences that can't be evaluated. They are the opposite of what you want to do if you want to decrease spending and increase efficiency."[55] In other words, it's just another Republican gimmick.

❁ **The minimum wage is a very destructive thing. We have a proven history of minimum-wage increases eliminating low-wage jobs. That works very, very perniciously against the ability of unskilled, untrained, inexperienced workers getting their start in life.**—Rep. Dick Armey (R-TX), January 1995[56]

RAPID RESPONSE

The best evidence from the best economists shows that the minimum wage is clearly a net plus for workers. For example, in 1992, when New Jersey increased its minimum wage and Pennsylvania did not, the only difference was that workers in New Jersey made more money. The higher wage did not cost them their jobs.[57]

EXTENDED VERSION

If anything, it's been proven that a healthy minimum wage is a good way of making work pay. Nearly two dozen studies have torn down the Republican notion that the minimum wage costs jobs. Just about every recent study that says anything other than that is in some way connected with the restaurant lobby, which hates paying its workers the minimum wage. Now, who are you going to trust?

President Clinton has proposed that we increase the minimum wage from $4.25 an hour to $5.15. That would mean a significant pay raise for 11 million people. It would be nice if we could raise it even more. Think about what it would be like to support yourself—much less a family—on $4 or $5 an hour. With forty-hour weeks, and no time off, that's $8,000 to $10,000 a year. Not much more than living on the dole, and that's exactly the problem.

SORRY, ARMEY

You know who Dick Armey is? Dick Armey is the Majority Leader of the House, one of the three or four most powerful Republicans in the country. He started out as an economics professor at a school called North Texas State, in a little town called Denton. Armey used to tell people about a mildly retarded janitor there at North Texas State named Charlie. Every day when Armey was coming out of his office he would see Charlie, and Charlie would keep the floors very clean. Armey and Charlie became good friends.

One day Charlie disappeared. Armey was worried. What had happened to his friend? The mystery was solved several months later, when Armey was picking up some groceries and ran into Charlie, who was there at the store using food stamps to provide for his wife and infant. It seemed that Charlie had lost his job because of one of those bleeding-heart programs, the minimum wage. You see, when Congress increased the minimum wage, North Texas State couldn't afford to employ Charlie anymore and he got thrown out into the streets. And this, Armey explained, is why he became a big opponent of the minimum wage and other similar bleeding-heart programs.

But David Maraniss, a reporter for *The Washington Post*, called North Texas State to check out the facts.* It turns out that the whole story was a bunch of Texas bull. The university told Maraniss that it *couldn't* be true, because everybody there is a state employee and the minimum wage doesn't apply to them. Then Maraniss started calling other professors who worked in the same building as Armey. Strangely enough, nobody remembered any Charlie working there, and nobody remembered any janitors getting laid off.

Armey's response was pathetic. He told Maraniss that a guy in charge of the school's physical plant—"his name was Dale something"—had told him the story.

Now, my question is this: If a man is willing to lie about a retarded janitor, what would he tell the truth about?

* David Maraniss, "Armey Arsenal: Plain Talk and Democratic Tales." *Washington Post*, Feb. 21, 1995.

PART 4: FLAT EARTH, FLAT TAXES

One of the things you find in working with public opinion is that if a politician does something stupid or greedy on a real small scale, many people will understand and even perhaps forgive. We can relate to minor stupidity and greed. We all engage in that type of behavior from time to time. We're human.

What people have a problem with is *major* stupidity and greed. That's what we're going to be talking about in this corner of the barbecue. Major stupidity and major greed from the Republican Party on taxes. Brace yourself.

. . .

If you ask people on the street which political party is more responsible when it comes to setting tax policy for the middle class, a lot will tell you that it's the Republicans. I didn't just stumble in from the sugarcane fields of Louisiana, so I'm not naive enough to think that I'm going to change their minds in a couple of paragraphs. But here's what we're going to do: We're going to look at the Republicans' first hundred days in power last year and what that time meant for the average taxpayer. After all, those "Hundred Days" were when the new House majority boldly explained to the American people what they stood for and then acted on those convictions. Why don't we just check on how those convictions played out?

Let's start with a little informal survey. When you're at your barbecue, ask all the people within earshot to think back to the Republicans' "Hundred Days," and, once they're in the proper nostalgic frame of mind, ask them if they've heard of something called neutral cost recovery. Somebody will probably guess it has to do with deadbeat dads or health insurance, but even when you hint that it's actually a tax provision in the Contract with America, you still won't get the correct answer. Truth is, only a handful of policy wonks and corporate lawyers know anything about it. It was the kind of fine print no one focused on. For the Republicans who stuck it there in the first place, that was the beauty of the thing.

So what is neutral cost recovery, anyway? It's a brand-new scheme for businesses to write off their investments in new equipment. Sounds pretty harmless, but wait till you hear how it works. It's the kind of corporate tax loophole that would have made Ronald Reagan's supply-siders blush. Let me share with you the first paragraph of an article on this little gem by the *Los Angeles Times* reporter James Risen: "Even most Republicans claim not to understand it, but an obscure provision in the GOP tax plan that appears headed for approval by the House today could mean an

SHIFTING THE LOAD

Fifty years ago, corporations paid 35 percent of all federal taxes. Today they pay only 11 percent. During the same time period, the share of federal revenues paid by individuals has *almost doubled,* from 48 percent to 80 percent.*

* *Economic Report of the President,* Feb. 1995.

---

enormous windfall for large U.S. corporations, create a new form of tax shelter and add more than $100 billion to the national debt."[58] And if that doesn't do it for you, here's what *The Wall Street Journal* had to say: "It probably would spur the creation of a new generation of tax shelters. And it could allow some big and profitable companies to escape taxes altogether."[59]

How does it work? My publisher threatened to withhold all royalties if I go into the details of inflation adjustments and opportunity costs. Suffice it to say that neutral cost recovery makes it possible for a company to buy a factory for $1 million and get more than $2 million in tax write-offs.[60] If you ask me, that's one hell of a strange definition of *neutral.*

When word spread that the House Republicans were going to go through with this, corporate lobbyists couldn't believe their good fortune. In fact, neutral cost recovery was so outrageous that most businesses were scared to push for it. They figured that once people saw what a corporate kickback this whole thing was, they'd have a PR nightmare. But guess what? For some reason, the public hardly made a peep.

It gets worse. Last April, right before tax time, the President sent Congress an emergency bill to help self-employed people deduct some of the cost of their health insurance. The bill needed to get passed quickly if it was going to beat an April 15 deadline—but that was easy. After all, it was a good idea that no one in Congress opposed.

The problem is, the Republicans acted like terrorists: They looked at the bill and saw a human shield. They figured that they could do just about anything they wanted to that bill without drawing a veto from the President. With millions of self-employed people hanging in the balance and the deadline approaching fast, the President wasn't about to shoot it down.

So what did these champions of the average American do to that tax bill? First, let's look at what they took out. In that same bill, President Clinton wanted to close a ridiculous loophole that allowed rich Americans to renounce their citizenship to avoid paying their tax bills. The President sure didn't think that was going to be a controversial move. I mean, it's not as if congressmen were getting a whole lot of mail in favor of greedy bastards who stiffed Uncle Sam by taking up citizenship on some island in the Caribbean. And besides, there were only about two dozen of these Benedict Arnolds out there—not much of a constituency.

But the Republicans in the House voted to leave the loophole open! I have no idea what they were thinking. At least with neutral cost recovery they could chalk up some IOUs with big business. This time, they were helping only a handful of zillionaire tax dodgers. Funny, isn't it, how the same politicians who had no problem with people casting off U.S. citizenship for money voted a few months later that it should be a federal crime to burn the flag.

Here's the other majorly stupid, majorly greedy thing they did with that same tax bill: As if a constituency of twenty-four wasn't small enough, they voted to give a $63 million tax break to one man—Rupert Murdoch, the billionaire media mogul. Congress wanted to stop giving tax incentives for people to sell TV and radio stations to minority-owned businesses. Except then they realized that Murdoch, who was nice enough to offer Newt a $4.5

THEY HAVE NO SHAME

You better be sitting down for this one. Last spring, the government of Belize wanted to set up a consulate in Sarasota, Florida. The State Department was sorta baffled. Why Sarasota, Florida? There was already a consulate in Miami, and Sarasota doesn't have a whole lot of Belizans.

But then they figured it out. Sarasota, Florida, is the home of the foam-cup empire of a man by the name of Kenneth Dart, who just happened to have taken up citizenship in Belize the previous year, presumably to avoid paying his U.S. taxes. The Belizan government was prepared to make Dart a Belizan diplomat and have him head up the new Sarasota post. You see, the only bummer about Dart's exile in Belize was that he could only visit the United States for one month a year without having to ante up all of his back taxes. As a Belizan diplomat, he could stay in the U.S. for as long as he wanted.

George Bruno, the U.S. ambassador to Belize, reported that Belizan officials told him Dart would live in Sarasota "with special responsibilities in the area of trade and finance." Dart would later help Belize come up with the money to build a consulate in New York City, where he "possibly would serve also as a consular officer . . . or special trade rep for Belize."*

There is some justice in this world. The Administration rejected the request. I guess Dart will just have to cross his fingers and hope a Republican wins the election this year.

* Al Kamen, "Belize: The Billionaire and Sarasota," *Washington Post,* September 11, 1995.

million book advance, would lose millions. So they—with the help of Democratic Senator Carol Moseley-Braun, regrettably—went ahead and made an exception for Murdoch. And then they killed the minority tax break for everyone else! I guarantee you one thing: Rupert Murdoch is one human being who won't say government can't work. For him, it works like a charm.

And now we come to what the Republicans in Congress—the folks who voted for the $100 billion tax boondoggle called neutral cost recovery and the $1.5 billion Billionaire Tax-Dodger loophole and the $63 million gift to Rupert Murdoch—have in store for the average American now. Be warned: No matter how stupid and greedy you think the Republicans were in their first one hundred days, you ain't seen nothing yet. What they've got in store now is going to kick about 90 percent of the American people in the teeth.[61] They call it "tax simplification." I call it "tax screwification."

You see, the Republicans know that they're not going to get into the White House in '96 just with attacks on "big government." That worked in 1994, when the attacks were vague. But now that the Republicans have put their cards on the table, and we see that "big government" is actually a code for Medicare, school loans, scientific research, and nutrition programs for pregnant mothers, the attacks don't look so pretty anymore.

So the Republicans had to come up with something new and fresh. They picked tax reform. Here's the snake oil: The Republicans want to scrap our entire 6-million-word tax code. In its place, they say, they'll give us a system everyone will love. They say it will reduce the tax burden for almost every American. They say it will save us billions of dollars and millions of hours filling out our taxes. They say it will raise our savings rate and therefore our standard of living. They say it will prevent the government from confiscating our money through withholding. They say it might even get rid of the whole damned Internal Revenue Service.

The plans to do all these miraculous things come in several Republican flavors, all of which people like to call "consumption" taxes. (That name reminds me of my great-grandfather's case of tuberculosis. But it's a free country; people can give it whatever name they want.)

The most popular flavor is the so-called flat tax. You've probably heard House Majority Leader Dick Armey bragging about it everywhere, since he was one of the first to introduce a flat tax proposal in Congress. The idea is to strip the tax code down to bare bones and then set a single, flat rate of tax for individuals and businesses alike—something around 20 percent. Armey claims that by getting rid of all kinds of tax deductions, like the ones for home mortgages, municipal bonds, and state taxes, not only would the flat tax raise the same money as the current system but it would also be so simple that people could fill out their taxes on the back of a postcard. Who could be against that?

I'll tell you who: people who make less than $200,000 a year. The problem is arithmetic. Let the Republicans talk about "fairness" until they are blue in the face; *the flat tax is going to raise the tax load on 90 percent of the families in America.* The whole thing is a huge scam. It's just like all the scams the supply-siders came up with in the 1980s. It's another Trojan horse—only bigger than anything we've seen before.

But when you're out in the barbecue trenches making the case that the flat tax is a scam, I don't suggest you use me as a source. I mean, my word is easy enough to dismiss. They'll just say, There goes Carville again. He's a demagogue. He spouts thirty-second solutions to complex problems. He is part of a profession that has demeaned the dialogue and discourse of the nation. He's a shrill, loudmouthed, vacuous spinmeister. He's a mercenary. He's a political hired gun with no convictions. No, sir, you won't want to quote me.

I bet if we put our heads together we could come up with a better source. Let's see. Maybe a college professor. Nah—they'll tell you that most college professors are liberals. Well then, we'll find a college professor who is conservative. OK, but what if that conservative college professor isn't from a reputable college? I mean, we don't want to take the word of a professor from some half-assed diploma-by-mail joint. OK, fair enough. Let's just think of some good schools. There's Harvard, Yale, Princeton, Stanford. Hold it. Stop right there. That's it—Stanford. We'll get the word of a conservative college professor from Stanford. But wait. What if that conservative college professor from Stanford isn't familiar with all the nuances of the flat tax? Well, then, we'll try to find ourselves a conservative college professor from Stanford who dreamed up the flat tax in the first place. Bingo. I think everyone would agree that a prof like that would be a reputable source.

Ladies and gentlemen, we happen to have not one but *two* professors who meet the above description. Please give a warm round of applause to Professors Robert Hall and Alvin Rabushka.

CARVILLE: *Thank you for joining us, professors. Let's get right to the meat of the coconut. Could you please explain to our patient audience out there in bookland what the flat tax means for average taxpayers?*

HALL AND RABUSHKA: *"It is an obvious mathematical law that lower taxes on the successful will have to be made up by higher taxes on average people."*[59]

CARVILLE: *What? Let me make sure I'm reading this right. Are you telling me that the flat tax lowers taxes on the wealthy at the expense of average people?*

HALL AND RABUSHKA: *That's right.*

CARVILLE: *And we're talking about the same flat tax that the Republicans claim would lower the tax burden on nearly all Americans?*

HALL AND RABUSHKA: *That's right.*

CARVILLE: *Thank you for your time, professors. You've been very kind.*

Straight from the horses' mouths. The professors slipped that "obvious mathematical law" into the 1983 edition of their treatise on the flat tax.[62] Take good note of this mathematical law—especially you in the media. And please don't say that James Carville said it. Hall and Rabushka, the guys who have been talking up this plan for more than fifteen years, said it themselves.

Let's see exactly what kind of numbers we're talking about:

HOW WOULD A FAMILY OF FOUR MAKE OUT UNDER THE ARMEY FLAT TAX?

Current Law

Total Income	$45,000	$85,000	$500,000
Adjusted Gross Income	$43,480	$82,090	$432,800
Taxable Income	24,460	56,280	376,000
Personal Income Tax after Credits	3,590	10,430	116,790
Corporate Income Tax	210	710	37,300
Total Tax	**$3,800**	**$11,140**	**$154,090**

Armey's Flat Tax

Total Income	$45,000	$85,000	$500,000
Adjusted Gross Income	$43,180	$80,700	$322,400
Taxable Income	30,980	68,500	310,200
Tax on Earned Income	5,270	11,650	52,700
Tax on Fringe Benefits	990	1,460	1,630
"Business" Tax	1,740	2,630	6,400
Total Tax	**$8,000**	**$15,740**	**$60,730**
CHANGE	*+$4,200*	*+$4,600*	*−$93,360*

Source: Citizens for Tax Justice. For Armey's flat tax, the analysis assumes that exemptions are set to be revenue neutral with current law.

Doesn't leave much room for hemming and hawing, does it? In fact, I'd have to say that any journalist who has written on the flat tax and has not mentioned the basic gist of Hall and Rabushka's "obvious mathematical law" is an intellectual fraud and a liar. And

THE FLAT TAX:
FLATTENING THE
MIDDLE CLASS

This is what the Department of the Treasury says Dick Armey's flat tax will mean for America: higher taxes, on average, for those who earn less than $200,000.

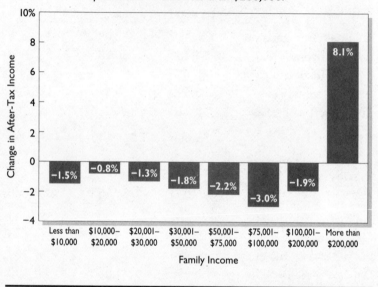

if you ever read anything from this day forward about the flat tax that doesn't include this fact, do not, I repeat, *do not* let the author of that piece anywhere near your wallet.

This is serious, folks. I am getting down on one knee. I am clasping my hands together in prayer. I beg you, in the name of all that this Republic stands for, invoking the name of the Pope in Rome and the Boy Scouts of America, please, please do not let any right-winger get away with saying a flat tax is going to cut taxes on hardworking middle-income Americans!

And remember: The right-wingers are lying when they call the flat tax an income tax. It isn't. *It is a tax on wages and pensions only.* The money people make on interest or capital gains will not be taxed at all. That's right! In the Contract with America, the Republicans were drooling over cutting the capital-gains tax rate in half. A flat tax cuts it to zero.

Let me illustrate. Take your average Republican fat cat with a comfortable trust fund of a million dollars. For argument's sake, let's say he invests that money in a conservative portfolio and makes about $80,000 a year in interest. With a flat tax, Mr. Trust Fund will not pay one red cent of that money to the U.S. Treasury. That's right—nada, zip, zero. Now, let's take a mail carrier who delivers Mr. Trust Fund's interest checks. He's had his route for thirty years and is now making a nice salary of $45,000. Mr. Mail Carrier will be stuck with a tax bite that's bigger than the one he pays now—about $4,000 a year bigger.[63] And remember: Mr. Trust Fund's not paying a thing on his interest checks!

Hardly seems fair, does it? In fact, I don't know how you could come up with a tax system more dead set against the 5/65 philosophy of valuing work. It says that the money you earn from the sweat of your brow is going to get taxed while the money people collect by playing the stock market is not. Pensions you earn from a lifetime of work are going to get taxed, and returns people accrue on bond investments are not.

But keep in mind that the flat tax is just one flavor of "tax reform" we're going to be seeing. In the coming months, we'll get more than an earful of bluster about lots of other Republican tax schemes. I've looked at all of them. Some are simpler than what we've got now. That I will admit. But what we might gain in simplicity, we will lose—and then some—in fairness.

I hope this tax debate sounds familiar to you. It sends shivers up my spine. *Trust us: If you just let us cut taxes on the rich, we'll all be better off.* Can't you just hear that familiar whisper in the background? Don't let them do this to you again!

And now let's try our rapid-response drill:

⚙ **The plan I have proposed is true to the idea of fairness we all learned in grade school: Everyone should be treated the same.**—Rep. Dick Armey, April 5, 1995[64]

RAPID RESPONSE
What I learned in grade school is that two people making the same money should pay the same in taxes. Unfortunately, that doesn't happen with the flat tax. A guy who gets a $60,000 salary will be paying taxes, while a guy who's making $60,000 from investments won't pay any.

EXTENDED VERSION
Another thing I learned in grade school: Slashing one guy's taxes and increasing someone else's doesn't count as treating them the same. Under Dick Armey's flat tax, families with incomes over $200,000 get an average tax cut of $51,000. Meanwhile, families making under $100,000 get an average tax increase of about $2,000.[65]

⚙ **We've got to overcome this mind-set in which we argue about everything in terms of rich against poor.** —Rep. Bill Archer (R-TX), December, 1994[66]

RAPID RESPONSE
Sorry, folks, but when it comes to the flat tax there ain't no other honest way to argue.

EXTENDED RESPONSE
Too many good Democrats get scared off the first time a right-winger starts accusing them of so-called class warfare. Come on! It *is* a class war. The flat tax is for rich folks. Middle-income and poor taxpayers are going to get screwed. Period.

None of this should be surprising. It's all part of the biggest scheme of income redistribution in a half a century.

Let's be bold for a minute and leave behind our talk of middle-class people. Let's talk about the poor. The scope of the Republicans' class war against the poor is truly beyond belief. I've got to quote an article by *Washington Post* columnist David Broder: "The conclusion is inescapable . . . the vital effort to get the budget back in balance is not an evenhanded, share-and-share-alike endeavor, but one that hits hardest on the most economically vulnerable and politically defenseless people in our society—poor women and children. How big are the cuts? Measured in constant dollars and over the same period of time, the savings projected in low-income programs like Medicaid, welfare and food stamps in the current Republican budget are seven times the size of those passed in Ronald Reagan's first Congress."[67] *Seven times Reagan's cuts!* These Republicans are making Reagan look like Santa.

❖ **We can unleash American productivity with a [flat tax], eliminating loopholes where millionaires now avoid paying any tax.**—Sen. Arlen Specter (R-PA), April 15, 1994[68]

RAPID RESPONSE

Let's talk about avoiding taxes. We currently have something called the alternative minimum tax, which means that millionaires and Fortune 500 companies can't skip out on paying federal taxes, no matter how many smart accountants they hire. The Contract with America didn't like that idea, so the House voted to get it off the books.

EXTENDED VERSION

In 1983, before we had the alternative minimum tax, 30,000 taxpayers who made more than $250,000 shelled out less than 5 percent of their earnings in federal taxes. It was much worse with American corporations. Something close to half of our largest and most profitable companies—including Boeing, DuPont, GE, and Texaco—paid absolutely no federal income tax in at least one year from 1981 to 1983.[69] Just wait. Thanks to the Republicans, we may see this all over again.

● **If history is any guide, the [Clinton] income tax rate increase aimed at the nation's most productive citizens will dampen investment, reduce national savings, slow business and job creation, and most importantly will fail to add a penny of revenues to the federal Treasury.**
—*National Review* editorial, August 23, 1993[70]

RAPID RESPONSE
As Ronald Reagan used to say, "There you go again!"

EXTENDED VERSION
I guess the *National Review*'s skewed history wasn't any guide. Since Clinton's tax on the richest 1 percent of the population was passed:

- investment has gone up 18 percent a year[71]
- national savings have gone up 18 percent as a share of the national economy[72]
- 1.2 million new businesses have started up[73]
- 6.0 million new jobs have been created[74]
- Treasury revenues have gone up by 13 percent[75]

Funny. I haven't seen these numbers in the *National Review.*

● **If you tax high earners at a higher rate, you are sending a clear signal that success . . . will be punished.**
—Mona Charen, *Washington Times,* July 12, 1995[76]

RAPID RESPONSE

If I have to hear one more op-ed writer or twerpy twenty-eight-year-old bond trader equating success with money, I'm going to drag him or her down to Louisiana. Miss Nippy will set that person straight.

EXTENDED VERSION

Right-wingers always equate productivity and success with money. I've got news for all of them. There are a lot of ways one can measure success in this world. Money is one way. And quite frankly, it's probably not the best. Look at my mother, for example. She and my daddy raised eight kids, and the way they put seven of us through college was with what my momma made selling *World Book* encyclopedias door-to-door.

I was the chief strategist in a winning presidential election. I get an enormous amount of money giving speeches. I wrote a bestselling book with my wife. I was the focus of a documentary that was nominated for an Academy Award. Not for one microsecond have I ever lived under the illusion that I was more successful than my mother. That would be a big mistake.

PART 5: THE "BIG GOVERNMENT" SMOKE SCREEN

You know what my favorite part of a barbecue is? I'll tell you. It begins when your host pulls out a ten-inch chef's knife and starts slicing up the watermelon that's been chilling all afternoon in the ice cooler. Man, there's nothing better. I always go for one of those middle pieces without a lot of seeds, and then I season it the southern way, with a dash of salt on top. No summer barbecue is complete without it.

Now, if you can make it to that part of the meal without having someone get in your face to spout off nonsense about our "big, bloated, unaccountable government," you're doing something right—or maybe you just forgot your Right Guard. Either way, don't think you're home free. If there is even a single Republican at that barbecue, you're going to have to deal with the subject of "big government." These days it's inevitable. You might just as well be prepared.

Forget about the watermelon for a minute. Walk over to the grill and lift off a nice, juicy medium-rare burger. You can put a sesame seed bun around it, but hold back on the condiments. Ketchup and onions and tomato would diminish the effect we're shooting for here. Good. Now you've got yourself an ideal weapon for the inevitable assault on you and the federal government.

No, you're not going to throw that burger at a Republican. Instead, you're going to use it as a prop. It just so happens that your average backyard barbecue burger is the ideal symbol of how dumb, dangerous, myth driven, and inconsistent these assaults on government really are. Trust me here. You'll see what I'm driving at in just a second.

Three years ago, a couple hundred people in the Pacific Northwest were eating hamburgers like the one in your hand and they got poisoned by a vicious new strain of the common bacteria called *E. coli*. At least three kids died. For good reason, people all across the country were shocked. They expect better than that from our meat supply. They expect that when they make up a hamburger on the grill or pick one up at a fast-food restaurant, the meat won't kill them.

So what went wrong in the Pacific Northwest? Wasn't the meat government inspected? Sure it was. All meat is government inspected. The problem is, the inspection process is outdated—basically, the inspectors just look at the meat and sniff it—and the meat-packers aren't willing to clean up their act on their own. To weed out infected meat, these guys need to bring in new scientific tests and modern laboratories. The old way just doesn't cut it anymore.

Now, some people would look at this situation and say, Let's fix it. That seems like common sense to me. We know the government and the meat producers have the technology to do it right. It might cost us a couple extra cents on a pound of meat. But I, for one, would rather pay $1.59 a pound for something that I knew was safe than $1.56 for something that might kill me.

That's the way the Department of Agriculture saw it, anyway. Even before the poisonings in the Pacific Northwest, it was working to set higher standards for meat and poultry producers and to modernize the inspection system.

But the Republicans in Congress didn't have much interest in fixing the problem. As you know, they think all new regulations—even regulations to save kids from dying from tainted hamburgers—are too much of a burden for hardworking American big businesses to bear. So the House Republicans voted in June of last year to block the whole USDA overhaul.[77] Sure, the new plan would prevent illness and save lives. But it's just more regulation, they said. And everyone knows that regulation is bad. Case closed.

Now, I should point out that it looks as if the USDA plan is going to go through and we'll get cleaner meat after all. Last summer, the Democrats in the House forced the Republicans to back down. But don't let right-wingers off the meat hook so fast. The Republicans did just about everything they could to trash the system and in the process made it clear that paying off their own campaign IOUs to the meat industry was more important than keeping your burger safe.

So, my friends, you have just seen how your burger can help you make the case that the Republicans' knee-jerk attacks on government can be dangerous. Now it's time to look at how that same juicy burger might help you make the case that these attacks are often based on outright lies.

I admit it: Even if properly inspected, burgers are not the world's healthiest food. In fact, if there are any health-conscious people among the Republicans at your barbecue (they'd be the editorial writers), they'll probably just have a piece of skinless chicken breast

FOXES IN THE HENHOUSE: INFANT FORMULA RIP-OFF

The government buys a lot of infant formula to help the mothers enrolled in a very successful program called WIC (Special Supplemental Food Program for Women and Infant Children). In the 1980s, the big three formula companies nearly busted the WIC budget by jacking up their prices dramatically. So Congress got smart. It passed a law— opposed by the big three formula companies, of course—to require competitive bids.

Last year alone, competitive bidding saved the taxpayers $1 billion.* States paid about 37 cents for the same cans of formula that sold for about $2.40 at supermarkets.† The savings allowed the states to buy food for an extra 1.6 million women and children.‡

The House Republicans weren't impressed. Or at least they were more impressed with the campaign contributions they received from the formula makers. They voted to get rid of competitive bidding when they folded the WIC program into block grants. Hell, what's a billion dollars a year in waste between friends?

And how did they explain this disgusting abuse of taxpayer money and the violation of every free-market principle I know of? One word: devolution.

* David Maraniss and Michael Weisskopf, "Food Program Defender Becomes Dismantler," *Washington Post,* April 4, 1995.
† "An Ill-Advised Welfare Reform" (editorial), *Tampa Tribune,* July 1, 1995.
‡ "Ending Bid War Feeds Firms" (editorial), *Houston Chronical,* May 6, 1995.

on their plates. That's smart. Too much red meat can eventually lead to heart disease.

Which is a big reason you don't want government red tape keeping any lifesaving cardiovascular medical devices off the market. In 1994, the Speaker of the House of Representatives said he had found just such a case. On *Meet the Press,* Speaker Newt reported that the Food and Drug Administration, the same odious government bureaucracy that wants to steal the cigarettes right out of your children's mouths, had "made illegal" a miraculous new heart pump used in eleven countries that "increases by 54 percent the number of people [who undergo CPR] who get to the hospital and have a chance to recover."[78]

Even I was appalled. The incompetence of it all! The arrogance! The FDA was just fiddling around while people were keeling over and dying!

The story was damaging politically. It had everything in it that the Republicans wanted people to believe about the federal government. Who's not going to hate a big, bad, bloated, regulation-laden government that keeps modern medical devices from hardworking Americans who ate a few too many burgers or who got stressed out at tax time and needed heart resuscitation?

But, lo and behold, Gingrich was dead wrong.

A couple of reporters made some calls and found out the truth about that heart pump: Independent test results showed that the device was of absolutely no benefit, so no one bothered pursuing it. No one had even applied for FDA approval![79]

Did Newt apologize? What do you think?

The revolution does not stop for apologies.

For our final burger-inspired lesson in "big government," here's another look at why these Republican attacks are so pathetically inconsistent.

You'd think if the Republicans were so damn eager to cut down the size of government, even to the point of sacrificing children's nutrition programs, then they'd also first go after every scrap of waste, fraud, and abuse they could find. Well, to put it charitably, they haven't. One of my favorite examples is cattle grazing. That burger in your hand, when it used to be part of a steer, probably spent a good deal of time grazing on federal land out West—in Idaho, Wyoming, or Montana. Now, I don't know how closely you've been following the pipe bombings and other violence in that part of our country, but suffice it to say that cowboys don't take too kindly to the government coming around, meddling in their affairs, giving them all kinds of city-slicker advice about over-grazing and environmental damage.

One thing these rugged individualists don't seem to mind, though, is a big, fat, porky government subsidy for their operations. They've got a mighty fine deal out there in cowboy country. The federal government only charges them about a quarter of what private landowners charge for grazing rights, and the Republicans even tried to sweeten the deal by dropping the fees altogether for some cowboys.

Some people, including the Secretary of the Interior, think this situation is kinda crazy—I mean, taxpayers are handing these people money to ruin our public land! What are we thinking? But when in 1993 the Clinton administration tried to use common sense and raise the grazing fees, the Republicans—and, in fairness, some Democrats—went ballistic and killed the plan. I guess the free market didn't look so good after all.

Right now we're protecting government aid to cows and at the same time we're cutting nutrition programs for kids. Cattle over kids. What the hell is going on here?

Look, the Republicans have some legitimate gripes about the way our federal government works. So do we Democrats. There's nothing in the Constitution that says we have to settle for third-rate services or $500 toilet seats. We can do something about it. We can set the bar higher and expect more from our government employees. We can bring in private-sector experts to tell us what we're doing wrong. We can drop programs that will never do much good. And, yes, we can ask state governments to do more.

But what we're seeing from the Republicans goes much, much deeper and meaner. We're not talking strategic cuts or increased efficiency; we're talking outright kills. Some would have us kill Food and Drug Administration, the most important consumer watchdog we have, because the pharmaceutical industry doesn't think it moves fast enough. Some right-wingers would have us kill the Federal Communications Commission because the $350 billion telecommunications industry wants to police itself. Some want to eliminate the Environmental Protection Agency because the big polluters think we should trust industry to do right by our air and water—just like they did in the good old days before the EPA was created. It's not just antigovernment.

It's antiwork.

It's antifamily.

It's anti–common sense.

Republicans will try to convince you that there's some kind of deep philosophical underpinning to their agenda. Come on! I'd say that there are deeper philosophical underpinnings to a case of indigestion. All they want to do is replace "big government" with big business. That's not philosophy, that's foolosophy. It doesn't take any deep philosophical underpinnings to gut our government. It just takes a willingness to let lobbyists rewrite the legislation that regulates their industries. It takes a willingness to make up regulatory myths when the facts don't say what you believe. It takes a willingness to abandon the federal safety net. It takes a willingness to raze instead of reinvent.

As every child learns in grade school, there is a fine system of checks and balances among the executive, legislative, and judicial branches within our government. What is often forgotten is that our country also depends on having checks and balances to control the power of big business interests. With a crippled federal government, we lose our most important counterweight.

Look, I wish I could say that what's right for big business is always right for America. Sometimes it is, like when a car manufacturer adds thousands of jobs to the economy. But sometimes it isn't, like when that same manufacturer is dead set against air bags, seat belts, and emission controls, or when it doesn't want to recall defective cars. We need a federal government that is powerful enough to take on big business from time to time. We need a federal government that is powerful enough to protect the interests of the powerless. That's what the Founding Fathers had in mind.

And now . . . well, you know the drill.

● **I think that we are absolutely bound and determined in this new Congress to make the effort to restore to states their sovereignty.**—Gov. Pete Wilson (R–CA), January 1, 1995[80]

RAPID RESPONSE

The Republicans don't really believe in devolving power to the states. The truth is that they believe in comforting the comfortable and afflicting the afflicted, and where the state is in a better position to do that, they're in favor of states' rights, and where the federal government is in a better position to do that, they're for federal rights.

EXTENDED VERSION

Let me give you just a few examples of where the Republican hypocrites voted to take power away from the states. First, there are securities laws, the laws that deal with sales of stocks and bonds. Certain interest groups thought it might be easier if they didn't have to comply with state securities laws, which are usually more strict than federal laws, and the Republicans were all too happy to oblige them and stiff-arm the states. They did the same thing on so-called punitive damages. It seems that big businesses didn't like states making them pay big awards when, through their own negligence, their products hurt their consumers. Not surprising. What was surprising was how quickly the committed devolutionists in Congress tossed aside the state laws and put a federal cap on damages.

❀ **The market is rational and the government is dumb.**
—Rep. Dick Armey, 1995[81]

RAPID RESPONSE
Look, is it rational that the meat industry would let tainted meat out the door, risking a panic that would cost it a huge quantity of business? Is it rational that the fishing industry in the Northeast would deplete the fish stocks and leave itself with nothing but old tires to pull up out of the sea?

EXTENDED VERSION
I just do not understand these folks who say that the market is the answer to all our problems. The market does many things well, but it is not always rational. And even when it is, we don't always like what it produces, such as monopolies, pollution, violence on television, and all kinds of short-term decision making.

❀ **Government bureaucracies in general are threats to everyday life.**—Rep. Newt Gingrich, 1984[82]

RAPID RESPONSE
If you ask me, the biggest threat to our everyday life is Newt Gingrich's mouth.

EXTENDED VERSION
If you believe Gingrich, I suggest you address fifty senior citizens and tell them that Social Security and Medicare are a threat to their everyday life. Or maybe you'd prefer to address a group of crime victims and tell them that the Bureau of

Prisons is a threat to everyday life. Or perhaps you'd consider telling the folks in Los Angeles who were devastated by an earthquake two years ago that the Federal Emergency Management Agency is a threat to their everyday life. What about the Army Corps of Engineers? The National Institutes of Health? The Centers for Disease Control?

✱ **Both the economic crisis and the moral crisis have their roots in the explosion of government.**—Sen. Phil Gramm, May 5, 1995[83]

RAPID RESPONSE
Let's get honest here about the so-called explosion of government. Are you aware that President Clinton has cut the federal workforce by more than 200,000 jobs and we now have the smallest federal workforce since Kennedy was President?[84]

EXTENDED VERSION
The big increases have been in state governments, which are only going to get bigger before the Republicans are voted out of office. From 1970 to 1992, the number of state employees increased by 65 percent, from 2.8 million to 4.6 million.[85] And here's another interesting little fact: Federal expenditures are a much smaller fraction of the total economy today than they were under Reagan, and they are no larger than they were twenty years ago.[86]

✱ **We believe you can trust the fifty states and the fifty legislatures to work together on behalf of the citizens of their states.**—Rep. Newt Gingrich, January 11, 1995[87]

RAPID RESPONSE
Has Newt Gingrich ever seen the Louisiana legislature in action? Take it from me: It's not pretty.

EXTENDED VERSION

Perhaps the Speaker has visited Orange County, California, where local managers blew billions of taxpayer dollars betting on obscure financial transactions called derivatives. I bet he has—it's solid Republican territory out there. He's surely seen the District of Columbia at work. It's stone-cold broke and begging the feds for money to meet payroll.

THINGS
GOVERNMENT
DOES RIGHT
❀ ❀ ❀ ❀ ❀ ❀ ❀

"With the exception of the military, I defy you to name one government program that has worked and alleviated the problem it was created to solve. Hhhmmmmmmm? I'm waiting. . . . Time's up."
—Rush Limbaugh, radio personality, 1993[1]

"Everything the government touches turns to crap. It's a reverse Midas touch."
—Paul Craig Roberts, former Reagan Treasury official, columnist for *Business Week*, 1994[2]

"[Everything the government does is] ripe for infection."
—Bob Dole, career government bureaucrat, 1995[3]

Does it scare you to think that many prominent Republicans now sound like members of an Idaho militia? It scares the hell out of me. The party has swung so far to the anarchist right that a reasonable Republican like Dwight Eisenhower simply wouldn't be able to recognize today's GOP.

It's hard to believe that only a few years ago we were having a fairly civilized debate on the best ways to slim down the federal government and make it run more efficiently. Now look what we've got. The Republicans just declare that the government caused all our problems and that every single thing it does is crap!

A BRIEF HISTORY
LESSON IN DEVOLUTION

Not only do Republicans make bad policy, but they put out bad history.

In case you haven't been paying attention, they are busy dismantling the federal government in the name of devolution. They believe that the federal government is incapable of doing anything well and that power and money should be turned over to the states.

We've had this discussion before.

In 1787, people in this country were just fed up. You see, they'd been living for several years under the Articles of Confederation—a confederacy of powerful states and a weak federal government. This arrangement led to chaos and unhappiness. Things were so bad they called a constitutional convention to figure out a new system.

We all know what came out of that famous convention—the same Constitution we live under today and "a more perfect Union."

You see, our forefathers had the wisdom to understand that we would have to accomplish big tasks and face powerful enemies. Boy, were they ever right on that one.

Can you imagine a loose confederation of states, each sovereign, none really required to answer to Congress, guiding us through the two world wars, the Great Depression, the Cold War?

Which state would have put a man on the moon? How many states would have guaranteed black people the right to vote? Which states would have had the courage and the resources to take on organized crime? Which would have issued the historic report that smoking is pretty damn bad for your health (North Carolina? Kentucky?)? Would all the states have cut in half the rate of poverty for their elderly citizens? Which states would have put up the funding to defeat polio? Which would have been responsible for building and maintaining interstate highways and waterways? Would you trust each state to make up its own rules regulating airports? Should we have fifty separate organizations ready to deal with hurricanes, earthquakes, floods?

Madison and Jefferson told the devolution clowns in their era to go home. We'll have to do the same. We are first and foremost a strong nation of *united* states, not separate states making up a weak nation.

Sorry, right-wingers. History *and* common sense are on our side.

So what happened? Well, the new strategy is a good way of grabbing votes, and it's a whole lot easier than engaging in real debate. They certainly don't need to worry about thought or facts or analysis. They don't have to come up with constructive ways of fixing problems. They just slash and let the government burn.

What really gets me worried is that if this nonsense goes on for much longer, it's going to turn into a self-fulfilling prophecy. Let's say the Republicans do convince the American people that the federal government could screw up a one-car parade. We'll never again be able to attract top people to government service. Who's going to sign up—or stay on, for that matter—when serving the country is a mark of shame rather than pride? And the way things are going, this is not just an issue of touchy-feely things like morale. In some places in this country, especially out West, you're already taking your life in your hands putting on a federal uniform or showing up to work in a federal building. Just think of how much worse it will get now that prominent spokesmen of the Republican Party are helping to turn the federal government into the great villain—the godless thug who wants to take away your Bible, your money, and your gun.

And then, of course, if the Republicans succeed in stealing all credibility from government, we'll get even deeper budget cuts than we're already getting, and no agency will have the funds to do what we ask it to do. Let's take the Environmental Protection Agency, for example. If the Republicans get their way, the agency's enforcement money is going to be slashed. It doesn't take a fancy computer model to know that the result will be more cities with unbreathable air and undrinkable water. Afterward, the Republicans won't take any responsibility for the environmental damage. Of course not. In fact, it'll be quite the opposite: They'll blame it on EPA's evil and inept bureaucrats, and they will have themselves another example of government failure. It's a win-win proposition. Gee, you don't think they might have figured that out already, do you?

I'd normally suggest that we fight fire with fire, but in this case that would mean lying or turning our arguments into absurd caricatures. But, hell, there's no reason we can't take Rush Limbaugh up on his challenge "to name one government program that has worked and alleviated the problem it was created to solve." And obviously we're not going to stop with just one example. Let's take a look at a handful of the hundreds of federal programs that have worked exactly as we wanted them to. Many of them are programs that the Republicans voted against in the first place and are now trying to hack apart or eliminate altogether.

I realize that some of you may hate the fact that we have to spend our time defending the idea that the federal government is capable of doing things right. I don't blame you. It's pretty embarrassing to think that we've let them go so far with their attacks that this has become necessary. But it's time to get down in the trenches and fight back with some government success stories. Better that we put some reality back into this thing now than wait until it gets even more out of hand.

Now, we are not claiming that the federal government always works. We know full well that the government, just like any business or family, has plenty of problems. But from there on we part company with the right-wingers. They say that all they can see is failure. We say we can see plenty of gems.

And when it comes to dealing with the problems that we know are there, we've chosen to try something we never saw during the twelve years Reagan and Bush were standing up there at the bully pulpit. It's called reinventing government. It means going in and radically rethinking exactly what we're trying to accomplish and how we're going to get there. Reinvention, in and of itself, has been a huge government success.

In fact, that's exactly where we're going to start.

Reinventing Government / National Performance Review (1993)

Last year, *The Death of Common Sense,* a book that laid out all kinds of regulation horror stories in the starkest terms, spent about thirty weeks on *The New York Times* best-seller list. You'd have to think that its author, Philip Howard, would be a good person to weigh in on the subject of whether Al Gore and his National Performance Review have achieved their goal of streamlining the government. Howard called NPR "a complete U-turn away from the reigning philosophy of government regulation."[4] He was right. So was Donald Kettl, a professor of public management at the University of Wisconsin, when he said that NPR could be "one of the three most important administrative initiatives of the twentieth century."[5]

This Administration's reinvention ideas have already saved the taxpayers more than $58 billion and cut the federal workforce by 200,000 workers. It's come up with another 180 specific reforms that will save us an additional $70 billion and cut at least 70,000 jobs over the next five years.[6]

But this isn't just about cutting costs. The main achievement has been making government work better. The Food and Drug Administration has cut the time it takes to approve drugs by a third. The Small Business Administration reduced its costs by 40 percent and cut its two-inch-thick loan application down to two pages. The Department of Housing and Urban Development is combining its sixty programs into three, improving efficiency, and saving $825 million in administrative costs. The Pentagon is bringing more common sense into its purchasing process. With all the old military specifications, even buying something as simple as cake mix was a royal pain. Now the rule is, Taste the cake. If it's good, eat it. If not, get another cake mix.[7]

So why hasn't reinventing government gotten more attention? Well, it doesn't make good TV. No matter how good the policy, using a scalpel is just not nearly as dramatic as swinging an ax.

Earned Income Tax Credit (1975)

The earned income tax credit reduces the tax load on working folks who make under $28,500 by giving them a credit toward the taxes they owe at the end of the year. It's designed to reward families who are working and keeping themselves above the poverty line. Understand that the EITC is an *earned* tax credit—as in, you have to *earn* income to get it. It is not a handout.

Here's something everyone should love. It gives 20 million families incentive to work and to stay off the dole. As I mentioned before, President Reagan was the program's biggest cheerleader. Sen. Pete Domenici (R–NM) called it "a great way to help low-income families with the costs of raising their children."[8]

But the times have changed. The Republicans in Congress needed money to pay for their capital-gains tax cut, and the EITC was just too easy a target. After all, not too many people who get the EITC have a lobbyist. So the Republicans voted to cut this tax credit back by $32 billion over the next seven years, raising taxes on 13 million working families, including 15 million kids. Read my lips: *That's new taxes!*

And how do they explain adding new taxes for the poor to pay for tax cuts for the rich? It's easy. Just listen to Sen. Don Nickles (R–OK): The EITC is "the federal government's fastest growing . . . welfare program."[9] You see, all you have to do is call it welfare and it's an easy mark—even if it's going only to people who are working and supporting themselves.

BAIT AND SWITCH, REPUBLICAN STYLE

In the early hours of a May morning last spring, I sat in McDonald's, drinking hot coffee and reading several newspapers—my morning routine when Mary and I are in Washington. That particular morning I read that Republican Rep. John Kasich of Ohio wanted to lead his party in taking on corporate welfare.

Gee whiz, I thought. These boys are on to something big. Oil drillers, timber companies, banks, airlines, pharmaceutical companies—the possibilities were endless. What a brilliant move. I was impressed, and, although I hate to admit it, I was worried for the Democrats. It sounded like House Republicans were dead serious about getting this done. We were going to be left in the dust.

I shouldn't have worried so much.

You see, it all depends on how you define corporate welfare.

Republicans said they were going after corporations, but instead they went after the American worker. The House legislation that was supposed to end fat-cat subsidies and corporate loopholes instead slashed the earned income tax credit and told corporations that want to dip into their employees' pension funds to go for it.

The earned income tax credit reduces tax payments for low-income families in the United States, helping them stay out of poverty. Is it me, or does raising taxes on people like this strike you as immoral and short-sighted?

And then there is the proposal that has pissed me off permanently.

Allowing corporations to raid pension funds amounts to letting them endanger the retirement security of their workers. It means that companies can take tens of billions of dollars out of pension accounts.* If the companies screw up and the pensions become underfunded, the federal government will have to come in and, using taxpayer dollars, clean up the mess.

So the next time some waitress cleans off your table or some guy helps you with your car at the service station, remember that's who the Republicans want to raise taxes on. When you see a retiree, say a woman who spent her life working as a secretary for the ACME Widget Co., remember, House Republicans voted to go after her pension. Because this just happens to be how Republicans define "corporate" when they say they are taking on corporate welfare.

* The White House, "Impact of the Republican Budget," Nov. 30, 1995.

Head Start (1966)

Head Start is the classic investment in people. The idea is to get kids off on the right foot with a quality preschool experience so they'll be healthier, smarter, and achieve more in life. And this isn't some Washington bureaucracy. Thousands of volunteers and community groups work hand in hand with local Head Start centers to help prepare these kids to learn.

Just throwing money at the problem? More than 200 studies have found that it works. Head Start kids are less likely to be held back in school, less likely to need special education down the road, less likely to create discipline problems, and more likely to graduate from high school.[10]

President Bush and a number of other prominent Republicans are big supporters of Head Start. But now it's time to put up the money for it, and the party has decided to cut and run—they've voted in favor of a plan to deny 180,000 kids the benefits of Head Start in 2002.[11] Not only the kids will pay the price of that kind of short-term thinking. The taxpayers will too, in the form of increased crime, higher medical bills, and less money paid in taxes over the kids' lifetimes. To call that penny-wise and pound-foolish doesn't begin to do justice to the matter.

THERE IS NOTHING
I HATE MORE . . .

than when right-wingers say, "It won't *solve* the problem." They do it all the time. We still have poverty, so big government didn't solve the problem. We still have pollution, so big government didn't solve that problem, either. Look, there are still Nazis in this world. Does that mean we didn't really defeat Germany in World War II?

AmeriCorps (1993)

In AmeriCorps, young people are given a chance to work together on projects to improve their communities—everything from ensuring neighborhood safety to building playgrounds. It's a great deal all around. The communities get help they would never otherwise get. The students get minimum wage to pay for their food and rent, and, after a year of service, they also get a voucher of about $5,000 to pay for college.

IBM had a team of top economists "provide a conservative assessment of rock-hard, tangible benefits of the program."[12] They found that for every dollar we invest in AmeriCorps, we get benefits of $1.60 to $2.60.[13] And that's just what we can measure in dollars. The economists were quick to point out that "the measurable benefits underestimate the total benefits to individuals and society." Gov. Fife Symington (R-AZ), one of the biggest free-market guys out there, loves the program: "AmeriCorps is not government as usual, but rather an investment in local programs—building public-private partnerships and delivering measurable, tangible results."[14]

So how do the right-wingers in Congress feel? After all, in the words of E. J. Dionne of *The Washington Post,* "you would think that a program that encourages Americans to do volunteer work, helps people go to college and disperses decision-making power from Washington to the states would be popular with the new Congress."[15] No such luck. Almost 90 percent of the Republicans in Congress voted against it to begin with, and now they want to kill it outright. The right-wingers just can't stand to think that Bill Clinton created a winner.

Federal Emergency Management Agency (1978)

Let me tell you the name of a person you will never find glorified in the media. He didn't go to the most prestigious school. You're not going to find him at a lot of Georgetown dinner parties. He doesn't get asked to editorial board meetings with major newspapers. His name even sounds a little Bubba-ish. It's James Lee Witt, and he runs the Federal Emergency Management Agency, the agency that helps people when Mother Nature knocks down their door.

It wasn't too long ago that Sen. Fritz Hollings (D-SC) correctly called FEMA "the sorriest bunch of bureaucratic jackasses I've ever known."[16] FEMA truly was one of the biggest stains on the federal government. In 1992, it turned in one of its worst performances ever when it took three days to show up to help the communities in Florida leveled by Hurricane Andrew.

Shortly after, President Clinton appointed Witt to head FEMA, and the agency has turned around completely. Over the past three years, FEMA has won universal praise for its handling of the Los Angeles earthquake, the midwestern flooding, and several southeastern hurricanes. In the words of the *Washington Monthly,* the reinvention of FEMA is "the most dramatic success story of the federal government in recent years. Not only does it provide further evidence that the government can work, it offers a blueprint for what it takes: strong leadership, energetic oversight, and, most importantly, a total reevaluation of its mission."[17]

When Witt took over, the agency was still spending a ridiculous portion of its time and money preparing for a Soviet nuclear attack. Witt refocused it toward dealing with natural disasters. He also brought in quality people. And he cut about half of FEMA's internal regulations.

No, Mr. Witt's not much of a hero to the pontificating editorialists. But to people who just got the hell shaken out of them in an earthquake or damn near blown away in a hurricane, he's a pretty important guy.

Clean Water Act (1972)

Twenty-four years ago, Congress passed the Clean Water Act to stop polluters from dumping raw sewage into our nation's waterways. Rivers were catching fire. People who went out on the Potomac needed to get typhoid shots. In 1970, only a quarter of U.S. river miles were swimmable and drinkable.

Thanks to the Clean Water Act and the Environmental Protection Agency, we've seen a dramatic turnaround. Gregg Easterbrook, a *Newsweek* reporter who has written extensively on the environment, has described our water successes this way: "Around 1970, the Great Lakes, Puget Sound, Chesapeake Bay, the Saint Lawrence Seaway, the harbors of Boston, New York, and San Diego, the Charles, Chicago, [and] Potomac [rivers] were pronounced 'dead' or facing mortality. Today these water bodies are biologically vibrant and showing annual improvement."[18] *Time* magazine says the Clean Water Act "has been a visible, undeniable success. Everyone benefits every day. Streams that were murky with mill waste and untreated sewage now are clear and swimmable."[19]

Don't expect the Republicans to be sending out thank-you notes to the EPA. They want to turn back the clock to the good old days when what you dumped in the river was your own business. Among other things, they would impose a twenty-three-step review process on all new environmental rules proposed by the EPA—talk about red tape!—and cut the agency's budget for enforcing environmental rules by a quarter. According to EPA Administrator Carol Browner, the "restrictions on our ability to enforce provisions of the Clean Water Act, when taken together, essentially shut down the Clean Water Act."[20]

Where did they come up with such backward proposals? They let the industries write the rules. Congressman Tom DeLay, known in the business as "the Hammer" for the way he hits on special interests for GOP fund-raising, turned to a group of a hundred lobbyists who call themselves Project Relief—don't you love that name?—to draft his legislation. DeLay's staffers even had the audacity to show a draft with a lobbyist's fax identifier on top of every page to a group of Democrats. Would it surprise you to know that these same lobbyists have donated more than $10 million to House Republicans?

Centers for Disease Control and Prevention (1946)

The Centers for Disease Control and Prevention, located in Atlanta, is the world's best defense against disease. As *Newsday* puts it, "To public health experts around the world, like Dr. James Le Duc, head of [the World Health Organization's] special virus division, the CDC is the world's No. 1 public health resource. 'The CDC,' said Le Duc, 'is the only ballgame in town.' "[22]

The CDC's experts are in constant demand all over the world. And its successes are legendary: It helped eradicate smallpox from the face of the earth. It helped banish polio from the United States. In the 1970s, it tracked down and stopped the spread of what came to be known as Legionnaires' disease. Three years ago, the CDC's disease detectives quickly figured out what new bug was killing people who ate at fast-food restaurants in the Pacific Northwest. Remember back in 1993 when people were dropping dead on Indian reservations in the Southwest? It took CDC scientists less than a month to solve the mystery—the culprit was a little-known creature called a hantavirus, which is carried by rodents—and stop the epidemic in its tracks. In the past two years, the CDC led the fight against the Ebola outbreak in Zaire—yes, that's the nasty virus that was featured in the book *The Hot Zone*—

A THREE-RUN HOMER

The government squanders our money? Well, over the past thirty years, the federal government has spent exactly half its money on three things: defense, Social Security, and Medicare. And what were our returns?

- *We won the Cold War*
- *We cut the rate of elderly poverty in half*
- *We gave our seniors the best health care in the world*

And was the price too high? Before you answer that, consider this:

- *Our budget deficit, as a fraction of our economy, is the second-lowest in the industrialized world (only Norway has a lower one)*
- *Our tax burden, as a fraction of our economy, is tied with Japan for the lowest in the industrialized world*
- *Our government spending, as a fraction of our economy, is the lowest in the industrialized world*

If that's not a home-run case for government success, what is?

---

and ensured that the plague in India would not spread to the United States. There are no greater heroes anywhere. As *U.S. News* reported, during that plague outbreak in India, the country's own doctors were fleeing the affected area, but the folks at the CDC "were begging to be sent."[23]

It's no accident that we're seeing all kinds of books and movies about disease outbreaks. The situation is truly frightening. In recent years, we've witnessed the rise of more than a dozen new deadly bugs—everything from HIV and Ebola to the bacteria that cause Lyme and Legionnaires' diseases. Ask any scientist, and he or she will tell you that as the world becomes increasingly interlinked through travel and migration, we're only going to see more of these killer bugs emerge.

The CDC has never been more vital. But owing to budget cuts, the agency has been getting only a fraction of the money it requires to improve its system for detecting new diseases. Its facilities are in serious need of upgrading. And its workforce, especially in the laboratory that handles the deadliest diseases, has been dangerously scaled back. The House Republicans want to underfund the CDC budget even more, and they even tried taking back money already earmarked for a vital new lab. If there was ever a case for building up a government agency instead of cutting it back, this is it.

Medicare (1965)

Medicare pays for hospital care, doctor bills, medical tests, and medical equipment for the elderly.

There is one health statistic that we lead the world in: Americans over sixty-five have a higher life expectancy than seniors in any other country. That's because 99 percent of our senior citizens get covered by Medicare. Before Medicare, more than half didn't have any health coverage at all.

Never fall for it when you hear the Republicans say they want to save Medicare. They don't. They don't want to scale it back either. They want to get rid of it. Exaggeration? Dick Armey, the Majority Leader of the U.S. House of Representatives, recently called Medicare "a program I would have no part of in a free world," and went on to say that he "deeply resent[s] the fact that when I turn sixty-five I must enroll in Medicare."[24]

In November 1995, the Republicans passed a plan to cut Medicare by $270 billion—at the same time they would cut taxes by $245 billion. The Republican plan means that seniors will pay hundreds of dollars more in premiums and receive less care.

Doctors made out fine in the deal, though. The GOP threw in all kinds of expensive goodies to the American Medical Association, just to get them on board.

Medicaid (1965)

Most people think of Medicaid as health care for single mothers on welfare. Wrong. Two-thirds of Medicaid goes to the elderly and disabled. It covers half of all people in nursing homes in this country.

The Republicans claim that they want to reform Medicaid. They say its costs are growing out of control. But keep in mind that spending per person on Medicaid is projected to increase *more slowly* than private health-care spending.[25]

So when the Republicans propose cutting $163 million from Medicaid, it isn't about controlling growth. It's about cutting nearly 8 million people off the Medicaid rolls altogether. That could be your grandparents. Now, can you afford the $38,000 a year it takes to keep them in a nursing home?[26]

And in one of the cruelest actions of the new Congress, Republicans in the House proposed to revive a provision that would deny Medicaid to people in nursing homes unless both the patient *and the spouse* had run down almost all their assets. Back in 1988, President Reagan agreed with Congress to repeal that requirement when he realized how much harm it was doing. As incredible as it seems, this new Congress makes even Ronald Reagan seem sensible and compassionate.

Meanwhile, turning back the clock and wiping out the whole program seems to be an option for Newt Gingrich. "We could wipe out Medicaid in the morning and say, 'Good luck,' " he told the National Governors' Association. "That's reality. It's historically doable. It's legal."[27]

Ban on Leaded Gasoline (first stage: 1975)

The ban on leaded gasoline has got to be a home run on anyone's scorecard. It is the "flagship" of all environmental regulations, according to economist Bob Hahn of the conservative American Enterprise Institute.[28] The results were so dramatic that environmentalists call the oil industry's endless stonewalling on this issue "one of the all-time corporate crimes."[29]

Doctors have known for a hundred years how vulnerable kids are to lead poisoning. Among other things, lead can cause mental retardation, low birthweight, and heart damage. Before the ban on leaded gasoline (and a ban on lead solder in tin cans, at around the same time), well over half the children in America had unsafe levels of lead in their blood. Within just a few years of the ban, the average level of lead in kids' blood fell by 37 percent.[30] The ban made perfect economic sense. The health and other benefits of the regulation outweighed costs by five to one.[31]

As Carol Browner and many others have correctly pointed out, if current Republican environmental proposals had been in effect twenty-five years ago, the EPA would not even have had the authority to ban lead from gasoline. Look, we're not talking about spotted owls and obscure butterflies here. We're talking about protecting our kids.

Ban on DDT and PCBs (DDT: 1972, PCBs: 1976)

Another regulatory home run. We all know that now. But we forget that, back in the 1970s, industry fought with every fiber of its being to prevent these bans from happening.

The bans on DDT and PCBs have made a huge difference for the health of birds, fish, and people. As Rachel Carson showed in her book *Silent Spring,* toxins dumped into our lakes and rivers were devastating all kinds of bird species. Thanks to the bans, many of these species, including bald eagles, have now recovered. As for humans, the toxins in breast milk have fallen by an average of 90 percent since the 1960s, and the amount of DDT in body fat decreased by 79 percent from 1970 to 1983.[32] Think Speaker Newt would have gone along with unfunded mandates like these?

Want more examples? Just flip to page 144. I decided to put about 30 more government success stories in an appendix for all of you hard-core types. Of course, even with the appendix, I've skipped over way too much good stuff. But think of it as a little way to give the government credit where it's due.

I'll just leave you with this last thought on the subject: Democrats do not object to ending up with a smaller federal government. That's what we're achieving. Thanks to a massive pile of debt we inherited from Reagan and Bush, our government is living beyond its means. We need to slim down.

What we want to prevent is ending up with a feeble, bad government—one that can't defend our interests around the world and can't protect and better the lives of our people here at home. Of course, people may eventually come to their senses and stop it from getting to that point. But I, for one, don't feel like waiting. I feel like taking matters into my own hands.

IT'S *STILL* THE ECONOMY, STUPID

❀ ❀ ❀ ❀

In an economy like ours, there are all kinds of trends. Things go up. Things go down. The dollar might be falling against the yen and rising against the peso. Housing starts could be picking up while auto sales are still slow. For most of us, these trends are the little stories in the morning paper we can skip right over.

But in this chapter I'm going to introduce you to two economic trends that you cannot afford to ignore—no matter who you are, how you vote, or what you earn. The trends I refer to are not just disturbing. They are the kinds of trends that can pull a nation apart at the seams.

Here's a quick summary:

Wages have stagnated or declined in America for the past two decades. The folks at the top have been making out fine. But the bottom 80 percent of the American workforce hasn't seen a pay raise, when you factor in inflation, since the 1970s.[1]

The wealth and income in this country is becoming increasingly concentrated in the hands of fewer and fewer people. By the mid-1980s, we had the biggest gap between haves and have-nots in the entire industrialized world.[2]

Before I get too deep into this, I should say a number of people have told me that wage stagnation and wealth stratification are too boring for this book. They say that just using those terms is enough to put people to sleep. The whole thing is dry. It's just a bunch of numbers.

I understand where those people are coming from. The media avoided this stuff for many years for the same exact reasons. But if this has to be a broccoli and Brussels sprouts kind of chapter, then so be it. There is no topic in this book that I feel more strongly about. And there is no topic in this book that tells more about the changing character of America. It helps explain, for example, why so many people feel like things in their lives are out of control. It helps explain why so many people are struggling even when the economy is growing. It helps explain why so many people say we've lost the sense of common purpose that once bound us together.

It also has a lot to say about which way we take this country. The nation has been on a rightward march since Ronald Reagan was elected President. What do we have to show for it? The wage and wealth trends show that a few Americans at the top have made out well, but the vast majority of us are going nowhere. In other words, it looks like when we have gotten economic growth in this country, the effects haven't been trickling down. By one estimate, between 1983 and 1989, the years the right-wingers like to call "the seven fat years," more than 60 percent of the new wealth went to the top 1 percent of the population and 99 percent went to the top 20 percent.[3]

Did you catch that? *Ninety-nine percent of the new wealth went to the top 20 percent!*

This isn't academics. This is life.

You know how people are always getting all misty-eyed when they're hearkening back to the decades after World War II?

CARVILLE'S LAWS
OF ECONOMICS

1. Those who say money isn't the problem have plenty of money.

2. Those who say stagnant wages aren't a problem don't have stagnant wages.

3. Those who say wealth stratification isn't a problem are sitting high up in the economic stratosphere.

When it comes to the economy in that era, it's hard not to get a little nostalgic. I can tell you this—it was one hell of a time to be growing up. After World War II, this country entered a period of unprecedented economic growth. Thanks in part to the G.I. Bill and a heavy-duty commitment to public education, this country built the largest and strongest middle class in the world.

It was an unbelievable cycle of prosperity. The more people who rose into the middle class, the more demand there was for the cars and appliances that other middle-class workers were producing. The economy just kept growing and creating millions of jobs. And best of all, everyone made out in the deal. In the three decades following World War II, the wealthiest 20 percent of American families saw their incomes double. So did the poorest 20 percent and everyone in between.[4]

But right about the time we pulled out of the Vietnam War, the economy started slowing down. A few years later, global competition started picking up. All the rules of the game changed.

Our economy stopped giving out A's for effort. Hustle and muscle didn't guarantee a lifetime job at the local plant. And the

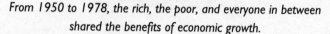

GROWING TOGETHER

*From 1950 to 1978, the rich, the poor, and everyone in between
shared the benefits of economic growth.*

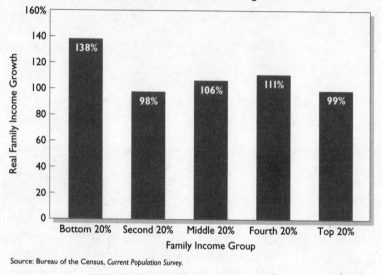

Source: Bureau of the Census, *Current Population Survey.*

plant manager couldn't expect regular raises or health insurance.
Pay stagnated, and we became the most unequal industrialized
economy in the world.

A few years ago, economists disagreed about whether wage stagnation and wealth stratification were actually happening. Could
millions and millions of working Americans not be making any
more money today than they were twenty years ago?[5] Could our
country really have more economic inequality than countries
where they've got lords and dukes? Even though the data were
there, these were not easy facts to swallow.

I can now report that there are no longer any serious economists who dispute these trends. It's just not possible. "Ten years ago, a skeptic could still question whether America was becoming a radically less equal society," the economist Paul Krugman said last summer. "But since then, the doubts of cautious economists have been swept away by an ever-growing torrent of evidence."[6] Look, I wish it weren't true. I wish the cautious economists had been right. But at least now we know. The smoke that we had been smelling all these years was a fire after all. Now we can stop fooling around and get busy putting that fire out.

GROWING APART

From 1979 to 1993, the rich got richer while the poor got poorer. (In case you were wondering what has happened under President Clinton, since his economic plan passed, we've started growing together again.)

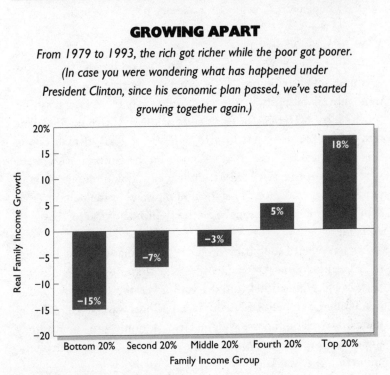

Source: Bureau of the Census, *Current Population Survey.*

There's just one problem. Even though nearly every single economist is shouting "fire," there are still a bunch of right-wingers who can't accept the sad reality. Or worse: Some of them accept the reality and say, So what? It's the single most outrageous thing I've seen in politics. The house is on fire, we're out there trying to put it out, and the right-wingers are buying marshmallows.

The marshmallow-roasting epicenter of the planet is in a place you would not expect. I just so happen to have its precise global coordinates:

> Latitude: 38 degrees, 54 minutes, 12.8320 seconds
> Longitude: 77 degrees, 02 minutes, 03.2666 seconds

Want to guess where this is?

I'd better give you a hint. It's in a building in northwest Washington—a building that is generally regarded as one of the more liberal outposts in the city. Still stumped? Are you sitting down? It's *The Washington Post*'s editorial desk. I have no idea why, but the people there just love to publish flat-earth denials of the wage and wealth trends. Not so much on the editorial page itself, where the paper has started to admit what's going on, albeit in an extremely lame fashion. They're almost always in the columns that appear, appropriately enough, on the right side of the spread—op-ed land.

In fact, when I look back on it, the thing that finally convinced me to write this book was one of those columns in the *Post*. It was back in December 1994, and the author was the *Newsweek* columnist Robert Samuelson. He argued that one way he knew living standards were on the rise was the fact that homes are "increasingly stocked with middle-class gadgets . . . 58 percent have telephone answering machines."[7]

I went nuts. I couldn't believe my eyes. Was this guy suggesting that answering machines make up for the lack of wage growth?

That the average working high school–educated guy, whose pay shrank by almost 20 percent during the past two decades, should be out celebrating that he can now get laid off in a recorded message?[8] This is better than Marie Antoinette. I can see the Republican plank now: "Let them eat voice mail!"

WHAT'S HAPPENED TO *THE WASHINGTON POST*?

Some of you may think I've tweaked *The Washington Post* too much in this chapter. Maybe I did. Maybe I didn't. But before you decide, check out the November 1995 issue of *The Washington Monthly*,* one of the most read and respected magazines in our nation's capital. Reporter Amy Waldman makes a devastating case that the *Post* has shown a stunning disregard for the working families of America. The personal histories of the *Post*'s most influential business writers and editors, she concludes, "show how a paper can lose touch with the average worker: Its journalists lead ever-more comfortable lives, with minimal contact with less fortunate counterparts, even as they succumb to the subtle pressures of their employer's own corporate self interest."

Howard Kurtz, the *Post*'s own media critic, told Waldman that he is often "amazed how significant wrongdoing by corporations is not always treated as a page-one story" and that "there's an unfortunate tendency in the media to do upbeat stories about which huge corporation is swallowing another huge corporation and, by the way, 10,000 people will lose their jobs." No major newspaper is as guilty of this elitist neglect as the *Post*. More and more of the *Post*'s coverage, Waldman says, "serves as a press release–based bulletin board for company profits, mergers, and personnel moves.... Vigorous consumer and corporate investigations," it seems, went out of fashion back in the mid-1980s.

And then, of course, there are all the *Post* op-ed writers who are out there trying to tell you that stagnant wages and our increasing wealth inequality are either a figment of our imagination or a good thing. Let me illustrate one reason why this arrogance kills me:

Let's say you had invested $8,000 in The Washington Post Co. stock in 1972. By the end of the year in 1992, that stock would be worth a cool $432,000. By December of last year it would have been worth $589,000.

In 1972, an average thirty-year-old high school–educated man was making $9,000. By the time he turned fifty, in 1992, that same worker was making $28,000.[†] When you adjust for inflation, the guy's making less money than he was in 1972. Let me repeat: *After twenty years on the job, his paycheck buys him less.*

A lot of people at the *Post* are telling workers that it's not a crisis that their salaries haven't gone up. Would it be a crisis if the stock market had been handing out stagnant returns for the past twenty years? How do you think that would go over? Food for thought, my friends.

[*] Amy Waldman, "Class, Not Race," *Washington Monthly,* November 1995.
[†] Frank Levy, unpublished calculations, 1995.

Another piece on my *Washington Post* op-ed hit list was by the famous George Will, who apparently is not in the slightest bit troubled by wealth stratification. In fact, in this piece I'm referring to, he came damn close to saying that this country could use more: "A society that values individualism, enterprise and a market economy is neither surprised nor scandalized when the unequal distribution of marketable skills produces large disparities in the distribution of wealth. . . . Promoting a more equal distribution of wealth might not be essential to, or even compatible with, promoting more equitable society."[9]

George Will is starting to sound like a character by George Orwell. The kind of economic inequality we have in this country is

AMERICA:
LAND OF INEQUALITY

America is now the most economically stratified country in the industrialized world:

1. United States	10. Luxembourg
2. Ireland	11. Germany
3. Italy	12. Norway
4. Canada	13. Austria
5. Australia	14. Netherlands
6. United Kingdom	15. Belgium
7. France	16. Sweden
New Zealand	17. Finland
9. Switzerland	

Source: Peter Gottschalk and Timothy Smeeding, *Cross-national Comparisons of Levels and Trends in Inequality,* Luxembourg Income Study Working Paper 126, July 1995. Inequality is measured as the ratio of the earnings of the worker at the ninetieth percentile of the income distribution to the earnings of the worker at the tenth percentile.

a nation-busting tragedy. Alan Greenspan, the Federal Reserve Chairman, is saying that it could be "a major threat to our society."[10]

William McDonough, the president of the Federal Reserve Bank of New York and certainly no one the Republicans could call a pinko redistributionist, goes a whole lot further. A little over a year ago, McDonough invited three dozen VIPs to the New York Fed's headquarters to discuss "the growing disparity in wages earned by different segments of our labor force." Without a hint of the usual monotone these Fed guys use to calm the market, he told them that the wage problem "raises profound issues for the

United States—issues of equity and social cohesion, issues that affect the very temperament of the country. We are forced to face the question of whether we will be able to go forward together as a unified society with a confident outlook or as a society of diverse economic groups suspicious of both the future and each other."[11]

Unbelievable! Even some Wall Street people get it! And you know that when Wall Street takes up the cause, we're not talking about some kind of Robin Hood fairness thing. As if they didn't make it clear enough themselves, they're talking about the possibility of devastating, long-term economic and social damage.

MAIN STREET'S PAIN IS WALL STREET'S GAIN

I'm no economist, and I don't play one on TV. (Does anyone?) But here's a simple lesson that I can't screw up. The key to getting wages up is productivity. In fact, there are few relationships in economics that are as tight as that between productivity and wages. When productivity goes up, so do wages. If productivity doesn't go up, wages don't go up either. Why? When workers produce more in a given hour, their companies can pay them more without taking losses in the process.

Over the last two years, however, productivity has been picking up big-time and the average worker's paycheck hasn't done much of anything. As just one more sign that Wall Street is clobbering Main Street, almost all the productivity gains are going into corporate profits. In other words, the worker is getting cut out of the action. This is not a good sign, to say the least.

I don't know if this situation will continue. But I do know that the Democratic Party should be out there screaming about this. If we don't, who will? Certainly not the Republicans. This is economic nirvana for them.

The journalist James Fallows has a good way of putting it.[12] He asks the following question: If you had a million dollars, where would you want to live, Switzerland or the Philippines? Think about all the extra costs, monetary and otherwise, if you chose a vastly unequal country like the Philippines. Maybe you'd pay less in taxes, but you'd wind up shuttling between little fenced-in enclaves. You'd have private security guards. You'd socialize only in private clubs. You'd visit only private parks and beaches. Your kids would go to private schools. They'd study in private libraries.

America is not the Philippines. And I don't think it ever will be. But if we keep going like this, Americans of the future will never know the kind of country I grew up in, where we rallied around a cause and had a sense of kinship. Sure, some people made more money than others. Sure, we had wealthy ranchers and poor share-croppers. Sure, some people shopped at the A & P and others shopped at the country store like the one my daddy had. But we talked about the same things. We went to the same schools. We shared the same experiences. All of these things are happening less and less and less. I hate to say this, folks, but if we don't already have a two-tiered society, we're sure as hell getting there fast.

So the question is: What are we going to do about this? How are we going to stop this country from splitting apart? How are we going to get wages moving up again?

Let me say in very clear terms that bringing down the rich is not the answer. Some of my best friends are rich people. Hell, I'm pretty well off myself. The problem is not that we have too many rich people or that the rich have too much money. It's that the rest of the country is standing still or getting poorer.

For the past decade or more, all of the economic gains have been going to the people at the top. But it doesn't have to be that way. At healthier times in this nation's history, we all grew together.

WHY STAGNANT WAGES ARE
EVERYBODY'S PROBLEM

Stagnant wages have taken a big bite out of the Treasury. You see, when wage growth slows, income tax revenues do too, leading to bigger budget deficits. According to Larry Katz, an economics professor at Harvard University and one of the smartest men in America, our budget would essentially be balanced today if real wages over the last two decades had grown just half as much as they did during the previous twenty-five years (everything else being the same).

The main answer to these problems is more education. As Labor Secretary Robert Reich often says, education is the fault line separating winners and losers. Most of the people who have skills that are in demand make out just fine in our economy, whether it's growing fast or not. It's the people who haven't spent enough time in class or in some kind of high-tech training program who are getting hurt.

Let's just look at the value of a college education. In 1979, the difference in pay between a high school–educated worker and one with a college education was about 40 percent. Now it's twice that, and it looks like it's going to keep on rising.[13] If everybody who wanted and deserved a college education was getting one, it would be hard to get all worked up about that statistic. But that's not the case. I know it's hard for professionals in the so-called BosNYWash corridor to grasp, but a lot of families just can't afford to send their kids to college. Since 1979, college tuition has gone up in real terms by about 80 percent.[14] And remember, middle-class wages haven't increased at all.

As every human resources office knows, we have a major skills gap in this country. Companies just can't find enough people with the right preparation. College is one way to get that preparation. But it's not the only way. For many jobs and many people, a better solution is job training. Most of our economic competitors, like Germany and Japan, figured that out long ago and have made a national priority of it.

So it doesn't take a genius to figure out that we need to find a way to make various kinds of education more affordable. President Clinton, who never once called himself the "Education President" but deserves that title more than any person who has sat in the Oval Office, has proposed a variety of measures. He would like to let middle-class families deduct up to $10,000 of the cost of tuition or training. He wants to combine seventy different job programs, almost all of which he inherited from the Bush administration, into a simple voucher so people can pursue the training or education of their choice. He proposed expanding the college grant program to include 800,000 more students by the year 2002. He created an outstanding national service program that allows students to save up credits to pay for college at the same time they're helping neighborhoods and communities. And all that doesn't even count what he's done and will continue to do for elementary and high school education. Let nobody tell you that this man is not committed at his core to education.

The Republicans in Congress have a different approach. I'll give them credit for creativity. Any moron could ignore the alarming economic statistics and just do nothing. But the Republicans aren't just any moron. They've found all kinds of clever ways to scale back every successful educational program we have. They want to cut 380,000 students off college grants. They want to kill off national service. They want to cut the job-training budget by $1.6 billion over the next seven years.

When you ask right-wingers how they can sleep at night, some will tell you that they're just eliminating fat and waste. The more honest ones will admit that these programs are worthwhile, but there's no choice but to cut them given the "current budget environment." Oh, come off it! These people have added $7 billion in military spending that the Pentagon didn't even ask for. They're for giving out $245 billion in tax breaks—most of them to the rich.

This is simply a case of criminally stupid priorities.

Even if we were broke, which we are not, this is the absolute worst time to be pulling back. This is the time to be juggling everything else so we can increase our commitment to education. Cutting education is eating our seed corn.

The biggest shame is that there are not enough people standing together to stop this assault. With hardly a peep from us Democrats, the Republicans—and you almost have to admire their skill here—have managed to convince people that America's biggest problem is the budget deficit. Hell no! Although we do need to cut the deficit, we now have the second-smallest budget deficit as a fraction of our economy in the industrialized world (behind Norway).[15] A balanced budget is all well and good, but not if it means we have to cut back on every means of helping to level the economic playing field.

We Democrats have to highlight the real problems: that most of our people are working harder and still barely making it and that we are splitting apart as a nation. I promise you, history will not judge us favorably if we let the Republicans go through with this without a major, knock-down-drag-out fight. These are not side issues. They are absolutely fundamental to what we are as a nation. If the Democratic Party cannot speak forcefully on them, we ought to just fold up our tent right now. It's that simple.

DADDIES MATTER:
A LONG OVERDUE CHAT
ON THE FAMILY
❂ ❂ ❂ ❂ ❂ ❂ ❂ ❂

Every family has to sit down from time to time and discuss sensitive subjects. My family does it. I'm sure yours does, too. It's like most things in life: The longer you avoid dealing with something, the more painful it is when the day of reckoning arrives.

The sensitive subject many of us in the Democratic family have avoided for too long is—you guessed it—the family. As some Republicans are very quick and correct to point out, the single biggest social problem we have in America is the breakdown of families. This is not an original conclusion on their part, of course. The person to whom we owe the greatest debt of thanks in this area is Sen. Daniel Patrick Moynihan, the scholarly liberal from New York who first sounded the alarm back in the mid-1960s. But fairness requires that I hand out some credit to Republicans, too—people like Bill Bennett and even Dan Quayle. Like Moynihan, they took all kinds of criticism, too much of it from good Democrats.

By now the weight of evidence in their favor is overwhelming. Without a hint of the usual academic hemming and hawing, the research shows conclusively that there is no substitute for stable, two-parent families. And believe me, when I talk about the research, I'm not referring to a bunch of right-wing pseudoscience.

I'm referring to rock-solid research done by experts of all political persuasions—and, yes, that includes a large helping of liberal Democrats.

I suppose we can choose to ignore this consensus and pretend that having so many kids growing up without their daddies has no social consequences. But let's get real. At this point, taking that approach would be no better than pretending that smoking doesn't cause cancer. Sure, plenty of kids from single-parent families turn out just fine. And some smokers run marathons and live to be ninety years old. But does that mean that growing up without a daddy or smoking a pack a day isn't harmful to most people? Of course not. The cause and effect relationships here are simply beyond dispute.

And please don't look at this as an issue that's confined to lower-income people caught in a "cycle of dependency." We need to face up to the fact that it just isn't an "us" versus "them" issue. It is an issue that touches every corner of society. We need to find ways to strengthen *all* our families. Studies by superstar researchers like Princeton's Sara McLanahan show that middle- and upper-class kids whose parents are divorced can be hurt just as bad as inner-city kids who never even knew their daddies. And if you want anecdotal evidence, go ask anyone who teaches kids, from nursery school on up. They'll tell you that it doesn't take too long to see whether any given kid from any given neighborhood or background comes from a one- or two-parent home. It's pretty obvious.

Our party shouldn't just be talking about this subject. We should be out there on some mountain screaming about it! We simply cannot prosper as a nation when we've got so many problems in our homes.

Why have we avoided talking about single parents and the importance of daddies? Well, we're a party that doesn't like preaching to people—you know, live and let live. But by letting the Republicans do most of the talking, we have let them own the issue. We have let them use "family values" as a way of bashing gays, working women, non-Christians, and the poor. We have let them use it as a way of tearing us apart instead of bringing our families closer together. And the whole Democratic Party has paid a steep price. We have all been caught on the receiving end of an uninterrupted barrage of silly-ass "family values" attacks.

If you think "silly-ass" is too strong, let me remind you what some of these attacks have looked like. Pat Robertson says this country's "ruinous moral decay and social breakdown" was caused by "a thirty-year war that the radical Left has waged against the traditional family."[1] Newt Gingrich runs around telling people that America's social decay is the result of "a long pattern of counterculture belief . . . deep in the Democratic Party" that has "undervalued the family."[2]

It gets worse. Gingrich suggested to the nation that Susan Smith drowned her kids in a South Carolina lake because Democrats were in control of Congress. (That, of course, was before he realized that Susan Smith's stepfather, a local Republican official and a member of the advisory board of the Christian Coalition, molested her on the same night the guy was nailing up Pat Robertson for President posters.)

The biggest victims of this onslaught have been the President and the First Lady. Holding up the banner of family values, the right-wingers have launched never-ending personal attacks on the President and his family. They have called the President and First Lady "counterculture McGoverniks."[3] And, of course, they have tried to turn out the bigot vote by calling the First Lady a "radical feminist"[4] who likens "marriage to slavery."[5]

The point is not only that the attacks on the party and the First Family have been utterly false, malicious, undignified, and downright unpatriotic. It is that they have been completely, inexcusably hypocritical.

I've had it. I cannot turn the other cheek. I've gotten both of them slapped so many times I ain't got nothing left to turn. It's time for a new approach. It's time for us to start giving the American people a peek inside the Republicans' glass house.

You see, the guiding spirits of the Republican Party—folks who are mighty quick to accuse the Democratic Party of destroying the American family and to preach about the value of tossing single mothers out into the streets—have not exactly been models of family virtue. Among many other things, far too many of them have left young kids behind after divorcing their wives.

The number-one family-values hypocrite who ever lived on the planet earth is Newt Gingrich. From now on, every time I hear him single out single mothers without saying a word about cut-and-run daddies, I will remind everyone that Gingrich left his first wife and his two teenage children. Every time he says that "any male who does not take care of his children is a bum,"[6] as he did in his most recent book, I will remind everyone that his first wife had to take him to court because he refused to provide adequate child support and that his church had to take up a collection to help his kids. Every time I hear him spout off about the President's marriage, I will remind everyone that the Speaker of the House of Representatives tried to get a divorce settlement out of his wife while she was lying in the hospital with cancer.

Let's do a study in contrasts. When the President and his wife had a difficult time in their marriage, they made a courageous decision: they decided to work through it. They talked openly about their problems and decided to keep the family together. As a result, Bill Clinton did not abandon his daughter. Chelsea Clinton comes home in the afternoon and gets help on her schoolwork from her daddy. When she goes out on Saturday nights, her daddy waits up for her. Chelsea Clinton is growing up in a loving, nurturing, two-parent family.

Newt Gingrich and a number of the Republican Party's other leaders talked the talk, all right. But when it came time for them to

CHARLIE AND THE CHOCOLATE CAKE

One Sunday I was kicking back with *The Times* of London, and I happened upon an op-ed piece that made the remaining hair on my head stand straight up. It was by the infamous Charles Murray, coauthor of *The Bell Curve* and now a driving intellectual force in the Republican Party.

What was so outrageous? Well, sometimes you hear right-wingers criticizing women on welfare without mentioning the role of fathers in the whole equation. In this article, Murray was much more direct. He said that the father "has approximately the same causal responsibility [for getting a woman pregnant] as a slice of chocolate cake has in determining whether a woman gains weight."*

This from a guy who divorced his wife when they had young kids at home. At least now I understand why the original Republican welfare proposals were tough on kids and easy on deadbeat dads.

* Charles Murray, "Keep It in the Family," *Sunday Times* (London), Nov. 14, 1993.

walk the walk, they walked right the hell out of their children's lives. Am I the only one who believes that a better example for the nation is a couple that has trouble and decides to stick together and raise their child together?

Before I end this chapter, I want you to know that I firmly believe that Democrats can take up the cause of the family and do it in a very positive way. I know that seems strange right now, when all we've heard so far is a message of hate from the right-wingers and when I've been pushing us to go into attack mode ourselves. But it is possible to bring up the topic of the family and make this a discussion that includes the rich, the poor, Christians,

Jews, Muslims, blacks, whites, reds, yellows, and anyone else who wants to participate.

Even if the right-wingers are still out there polarizing people with their attacks, and even if we have to spend some of our time exposing their hypocrisy in an aggressive way, we can lend a voice of sanity to this issue. We can calmly explain why all the talk of personal responsibility doesn't go very far if we are intent on kicking away the very props that families desperately need in order to make ends meet. I'm talking about funding for education. I'm talking about help with health care and child care. I'm talking about tax credits for working families struggling near the poverty line. I'm talking about a minimum wage that would allow a daddy or a mommy to support a child.

Labor Secretary Reich summed it up better than anyone:

> We honor family values every time we create a job. We honor family values every time children have a safe place to go when their parents are at work. We honor family values every time we secure a working person's pension. We honor family values every time we teach a child to learn. We honor family values every time we move a young mother from welfare to work, or help a worker get better skills, or help someone who has lost a job to find a new one.[8]

Family values is about lending a helping hand, not a swinging foot, to those who are down. It is about paychecks. It is about security. It is about hope.

And, yes, it does involve preaching about morals. But we've had more than enough religion of division. Let's tone down on the fire and brimstone and pump up the compassion and support. Again, there is a positive way to do this. We should have figured that out long ago.

THEY CALL ME
MR. CARVILLE

❋ ❋ ❋ ❋ ❋ ❋ ❋

Back in 1969, I worked as a teacher at a middle school for boys in South Vacherie, Louisiana. I taught science in a classroom that backed right up against a sugarcane field. I didn't have any formal training as a teacher, and it took me until about March to figure out where the small public school kept the extra staplers and the good kind of chalk. But I did bring one piece of wisdom to my job. It was something I had learned from my own undistinguished but memorable career as a student: While not every good disciplinarian is a good teacher, every bad disciplinarian is a bad teacher.

I was fresh out of the Marine Corps, and I ran my classroom the way my sergeant had run our platoon.

Before I sat down to write this chapter, we called a number of my former students to find out what, if anything, they remembered from those long-ago days. Without exception, they all remembered the Equalizer. The Equalizer was a long aluminum pointer, especially useful for rapping the underside of a student's desk during the execution of a one-on-one pop quiz. It must have left quite an impression, because they still won't call me anything but Mr. Carville.

You know, it's funny, I thought they'd do a lot of talking about how small and hot the classrooms had been, or that it was the first year of integration, or that there were no girls. But instead, after they were done talking about the Equalizer, most of them brought up how much I had expected of them and how hard I had pushed them to learn. We spent a lot of time talking about where they were headed.

I guess I taught them a lot about life, but I learned a lot, too. Most of all, I figured out how much parents count. You can stand up there in front of the blackboard for as long as you want, but the kids who do well in your class are going to be the ones whose folks supervise their homework and set limits on their television. The same parents who show up on Meet-the-Teacher Night to squeeze into those little desks and ask questions about what their kids are learning and how they're doing. The same parents who begin reading bedtime stories the day their babies come home from the hospital.

I'm not talking about a revolutionary formula for success here. We know what works. Our kids need classrooms in which breaking the rules has real and predictable consequences. They need teachers who not only believe they can make great strides but expect them to. They need to know that hard work yields results to be proud of. And they need parents who give a damn.

So where does the federal government come into all this? We sure as hell can't pass a law that compels parents to recite Mother Goose to their three-year-olds or spend more time on math problems with their second-graders. And school reform is fundamentally a state and local issue. But there are some things that the folks in Washington can do to make a difference in the classroom. We can encourage local school districts to raise academic standards and spell out what is expected of kids in each grade—and then provide the research and start-up money to design strategies for helping kids achieve these goals. We can provide grants for teacher education and training. We can help communities keep drugs and violence out of their schools, so that our classrooms are places where teachers can teach and students can learn. Again, not rocket science. Just common sense.

It just so happens we have a new law on the books designed to do exactly these things: It's called Goals 2000.

The concept for this piece of legislation originated with Republican President George Bush. Bush got all the nation's governors together on a fall day in 1989 in Charlottesville, Virginia. This was no touchy-feely kind of gathering; they knew we needed to make our kids, our schools, and our country more competitive. With Governor Clinton of Arkansas playing a key role, they hammered out an agreement to raise standards and ask more of our kids than ever before.

George Bush didn't get a chance to see this plan through Congress, but when Bill Clinton took office, he took the ball and ran with it. He signed Goals 2000 into law on March 31, 1994. It was a huge day in American education and truly a bipartisan victory. Goals 2000 had been endorsed, supported, and praised by Democrats, Republicans, business leaders, grassroots activists, teachers, and parents alike. The leaders of communities across the nation had come together and done what was right for America's kids.

Sound like a fairy tale? Like it's too good to be true?

You're right. It is.

At least, too good to last. Because several months later, Republicans took control of Congress. These guys knew they owed their victories to the activism of their party's wing nuts—wing nuts who just happen to hate Goals 2000. The Republicans were only too happy to offer up the new program as a sacrificial lamb.

These partisans did, however, have to figure out a way to say they were for education but against the President's plan. You're not going to get a member of Congress to admit he or she is not for education—it would be like saying that you don't know the words to the Pledge of Allegiance, or that you think America would be just fine without baseball. And they couldn't say Goals

2000 was breaking the bank—it's annual cost is less than thirty bucks per kid. They couldn't say it represented the intrusive heavy hand of government—it's just a funding mechanism (no strings attached) for ideas and proposals that come from the local level. They couldn't say it was filled with goofy liberal stuff like Cross-cultural Transoceanic Appreciation Week because it emphasizes achievement in the basics, like reading and math. They couldn't say it would pile up reams of paperwork because it adds no new regulations, and the application for funding is only four pages long. They couldn't say it was an unfunded mandate because it is funded, and, what's more, it's not a mandate—participation by schools and states is entirely voluntary.

The truth clearly wasn't going to work, so they ignored it and cranked up the myth machines.

For starters, Republicans have turned everything on its head. Instead of recognizing that Goals 2000 encourages local innova-tion, they have painted a picture of top-down, Big Brother man-agement: Uncle Sam peeking into every classroom in every schoolhouse in America.

While campaigning in New Hampshire, Republican presiden-tial hopefuls, including former Education Secretary Lamar Alexander, go out of their way to applaud that state's decision to reject Goals 2000 money for their schools. Why didn't New Hampshire join the forty-seven states that applied for the funding? Well, after all, think of what Goals 2000 might lead to. Gun groups protested that the program would allow the feds to remove kids from homes where parents own guns that can be loaded in ten minutes (who knows where they dug that up; Goals 2000 just says schools should be gun-free). Others feared that a United Nations cabal was at work and that school inoculation programs would lead to injections of mind-controlling substances (I'm not even going to touch that).[1]

Instead of consulting with the folks at Oregon's Department of Education, who say Goals 2000 "has given us flexibility that we've never enjoyed,"[2] or listening to the president of Maryland's board of education, who said, "We've had no experience with any federal restrictions or oversight,"[3] New Hampshire's educators must have consulted with the woman who claimed before the Montana Militia that she was turned into a "Goals 2000 sex slave."[4]

I hate that the kids in New Hampshire's public schools have lost out because hysterics control the agenda. But to be honest, I'm not all that surprised by the venom and the stupidity. Right-wingers don't want public education to succeed. Sound like an exaggeration? Listen to this:

> You want to solve the education crisis? Then get the government out of it. Privatize it. All the way. One hundred percent. I'm serious . . . How long are we going to tolerate what's going on? Oh, you can't find a school? Oh, we abolished all your schools, you can't find one? Then home school. Teach your kids at home.[5]

Those visionary lines helped earn their speaker a standing ovation at a recent Christian Coalition gathering. Oh, those are just the wackos, you're thinking. But, hey, that speaker was sandwiched in between a couple of major presidential hopefuls, who, in their own speeches, gave new meaning to the word *pander*.

Goals 2000 isn't the only thing on their chopping block; Republicans are trying to gut every major education program. It's a hell of a way to prepare for the future: Nearly 200,000 toddlers won't be getting the benefits of Head Start, and millions of kids will find vital college-loan programs decimated. At a time when our changing economy will demand more and more of our young people, the support they need will be yanked out from under them. Using tax dollars for public education just doesn't seem to hold much sway with the GOP.

Well now, how about tax dollars for private education?

Ahhh, now you're talking. That's what these voucher schemes, long the favorites of the Republican Party, are all about: using *your* tax dollars to pay for all or part of the private school education some parents choose for their kids.

Let me say right off the bat that I have nothing against private or parochial education. In fact, as you read this, some dedicated nuns in Louisiana are busy making an indelible impression on most of my twenty nieces and nephews. And while both my mother and I have taught in public schools, two of my sisters teach at parochial schools. I myself graduated, if just barely, from a Catholic school. But I can think of some pretty good reasons why vouchers for private schools are a bad idea.

First of all, and probably most important, these schemes deprive public schools of the support they deserve. Parents who choose to send their kids to private school still have a responsibility to support public education, not the other way around. Pat Robertson, one of the biggest endorsers of voucher schemes, has said: "They say vouchers would spell the end of public schools in America. To which we say, so what?"[6] What in the world is he thinking? Look, 42 million of our kids go to public school each day.[7] Their future is America's future. No matter what we choose for our own kids, we all have a stake in the success of public education.

There's something else I want you to understand: Just because vouchers are public money doesn't mean that the participating private schools will be accountable to the public. Wondering about the curriculum at the David Koresh Academy? How about the expulsion policy at the Louis Farrakhan School? Well, stop wondering. It ain't any of your business now, and it will never get to be your business, even if they used your tax dollars to send somebody to these schools.

Need another reason to give voucher plans a big thumbs-down? How about the fact that they simply don't work. You see, the whole idea behind vouchers is that private schools do a better job of educating kids. Only they don't.

Look what happened in Milwaukee, where they've been trying this voucher thing for four years now. The students who used vouchers to switch from public schools to private schools didn't learn a damn thing more than the kids who stayed put. Math scores? No change. Reading scores? No change.[8]

Whenever I hear people say that private schools do a better job than public schools, I tell them what Lester Maddox, the former governor of Georgia, said when someone complained about the sorry condition of his state's prisons: "Then give me a better class of inmate." Because the truth of the matter is, public schools don't get to choose their students any more than the state of Georgia gets to pick and choose its prisoners.

Have you ever heard of Thomas Jefferson High School in Fairfax County, Virginia? It's a public school, but it ain't just any public school—it's called a "magnet school," and it *does* get to choose its students. Thomas Jefferson admits only the highest performing kids around, and it is unbelievably tough to get into. And for six years in a row, it has produced more National Merit semifinalists than any other high school in the nation.[9] That's a mighty impressive record—one that suggests that if public schools had to educate only the brightest students, they could do as well or better than the best private schools.

Of course, private schools always get to choose their students. Before gaining admission, kids usually face a gauntlet of entrance exams and interviews. Academic records are checked, recommendations are required. Disabled in any way? How's your English? Problems at home? Ever been in any trouble? Many of our children shouldn't expect a warm welcome, or any welcome at all, for that matter, at most private schools. Many of the kids in Milwaukee who received vouchers couldn't find a private school that would accept them.[10] Guess where they went? That's right, back to the public schools. I guess they haven't ironed out all the wrinkles in this voucher idea yet. You ain't going to see kids from the South Bronx showing up at Manhattan's fancy Dalton School too soon.

So when people hold up vouchers as the way to fix what's wrong with education today, tell them you're not so sure you want to spend your tax dollars to subsidize private education. Tell them you'd rather use that money to make our public schools stronger.

Tell them that vouchers aren't an answer—they're a gimmick.

Unfortunately, vouchers aren't the only bad idea on the educational "reform" scene. They're joined by the stellar notion of hiring profit-making companies to take over our public schools.

Ever heard of Educational Alternatives, Inc.? It's the Minnesota-based company at the forefront of this school-privatization movement. Let's take a quick look at its track record.

A couple of years ago, EAI told Baltimore that it could do a better job of running the city's public schools. It got a contract from Baltimore to run nine of them—and $18 million more than the city was planning to spend on those schools.[11] The company was going to come in and clean things up. And you know what? The schools did get cleaner. But the first two years of this privatization experiment had some other results, too: Test scores for kids at the nine EAI schools dropped, while at the same time they rose for kids in other Baltimore city schools.[12] Special-education programs were nearly dismantled when EAI fired half of the qualified teachers.[13] EAI schools lagged behind the attendance improvements made in the rest of the city's schools.[14] And, more recently, an independent study by the University of Maryland concluded this: EAI was spending more money per kid than other Baltimore public schools, but the EAI kids weren't achieving more.[15] Three and a half years into the five-year contract, the school board in Baltimore voted unanimously to dump EAI.

Like Baltimore, Hartford was a school district with big troubles that found EAI's sales pitch too tempting to turn down. In 1994, it went ahead and hired EAI to manage all thirty-two of its schools and oversee its $200 million budget.[16]

Part of the deal was that the company would get to keep half of any of the money it could "save" (read: cut).[17] One budget submitted by EAI called for firing almost 300 teachers[18]—probably not the smartest way of relieving overcrowded classrooms. This is the same company that planned to have the city cough up $1.2 million for expenses for its top executives.[19] These were only two of the reasons why Hartford decided to take back control of twenty-six of their thirty-two schools from EAI.[20] Better late than never.

So here's a piece of sage advice for other school districts around the country: Next time you want cleaner playgrounds and better-kept classrooms, hire a couple of extra janitors. But don't blow millions on a company that can't deliver much else. Companies like EAI have one bottom line, and believe me, it isn't the well-being of our kids.

School districts in America need to stop shopping for quick fixes and start looking for real answers. One place they might want to begin is in the nation's largest public school system, New York City.

Now I know what you're thinking. Crumbling school buildings with no Bunsen burners, no microscopes, no fancy computers. Too much bureaucracy. Overcrowded classrooms. Not enough textbooks. High absenteeism. Tough neighborhoods and even tougher kids.

And those were only some of the problems faced by the brilliant educator Ramon Cortines when he was the chancellor of public schools in New York. You know what his response was? He called for higher standards and a tougher curriculum. That's right. This guy spent hours every day in these schools, talking to principals and teachers and kids, and he never stopped believing that the answer was to expect more: He said, "The worst thing we can do for our students, the most insidious way of cheating them, the surest formula for failure is to ask little and expect little of our students."[21]

I'm right there with Mr. Cortines on this one. It's human nature not to stretch much further than you're expected to. If parents or teachers set the bar at five feet, kids will usually clear it by a quarter inch. But if the bar is set at only four feet, they'll never make it to five. As long as they know where the bar is, they'll make it over. The idea is to set it at a level where they have to give all they can.

And that's what Ramon Cortines did when he required every high school student in the city's public schools to take college-prep math and science courses instead of settling for what he called "bonehead" math classes, where students learned how to make change and balance a checkbook. The result? Some kids failed, but thousands more passed these tougher courses.[22]

Cortines told his schools to expect more from their younger kids, too. The result? If you read *The New York Times* on June 13, 1995, you may have noticed the following item:

> Elementary school students in all thirty-two New York City School districts raised their math and reading test scores this spring for the first time in six years. . . . The achievement is a significant one for the nation's largest school system, which last year absorbed $540 million in budget cuts. . . . School officials attributed the overall improvement to a new curriculum framework, a new set of guidelines for what children should learn and when they should learn it.[23]

Now, I'm not saying we all should rush out and enroll our kids in New York City's public schools. Lord knows, the educators in that city are fishing in some pretty troubled waters. My point is that in the face of some of the toughest problems a school system can encounter, they had the courage to respond with good old-fashioned common sense. Instead of turning the schools over to companies out to make a buck, instead of funneling public money to private academies, they told their kids to try harder and do more. The results speak for themselves.

I suggest you check out the next local school board meeting in your area and ask the powers that be a simple question: If New York can do it, why can't we?

There are two things we can say about public education in America with absolute certainty. Number one: There are problems. Everybody says this, and everybody's right. Number two: We're making progress. Too few people have said it. I just did. And I'm right, too.

More of our kids are taking the tougher courses that will prepare them for college. Math and science scores are up. More high school students are going on to college. We're starting to turn the corner.

We shouldn't forget about the very real problems our public schools face every day, but we ought to think pretty seriously about the message we send our kids. I mean, should we tell them that they attend decaying, dangerous, going-nowhere-fast dumps? Or should we highlight their achievements, tell them when they've done a good job, and show them where there's room to improve? That's a no-brainer, Uncle James, my nephews would say to me. And they'd be right.

Because nothing is more important to our nation's future than seeing that all Americans have the skills and the education they need to succeed in the new rapidly changing economy. And that means making sure not only that higher education is affordable but that our elementary, middle, and high schools are serving up both high expectations and hope.

Republicans in Congress would have you believe that gutting education is something we all have to accept, a necessary price for their tax cuts and balanced budget. But look, we aren't talking about unnecessary government pork here: In fact, the Clinton administration has eliminated one-third of the federal educational regulations that it inherited. We're not talking about extras. We're talking about keeping violence and drugs out of our classrooms. We're talking about increasing accountability and innovation for our schools at the local level. We're talking about making sure the door to a college education isn't slammed shut for those who can't afford rising tuition costs. This is where the rubber meets the road. And if the Republican leadership truly had our kids' best interest at heart, they would pay less attention to right-wingers like Pat Robertson and Phyllis Schlafly and more to the tradition represented by Republicans like Congressman Justin Smith Morrill.

You haven't heard of Mr. Morrill, you say? Let me share with you a little history.

In 1862, things were not going so well for the Union. There were big-time money problems, and they were losing a war to boot. General Lee was kicking some serious butt. And this man by the name of Morrill—a Republican from Vermont—introduced a bill in Congress. He said, "We're going to have land-grant universities in this country—one for every state—to give Americans opportunities for training and learning."

And they said, "Man, you must be crazy, we're in the middle of a civil war. Building new universities? What the hell are you thinking?"

But he persisted, and eventually, during this country's darkest hour, President Lincoln signed the Morrill Act into law. I think we can all agree that Congressman Morrill knew a good investment when he saw one. At that time, building those schools meant American workers could get an agricultural and technical education. Today, land-grant colleges and universities—schools like Cornell, the University of Kentucky, MIT, Purdue, and the University of Vermont—count millions of Americans as their alums (Presidents, members of Congress, CEOs, and Nobel Prize winners among them).[24]

I say if this country had the guts to invest in education at that time, we need to get busy now. I don't know about you, but I'm not going to sit back quietly and watch shortsighted Republicans make education less affordable and less accessible. We've got to have the same vision, the same courage, the same perseverance that Justin Smith Morrill had.

Today our federal government plays, and must continue to play, a crucial role in helping our youngest kids get a head start on learning, in aiding those communities who are working to make their schools better, and in driving down the cost of higher education.

Five/65 Democrats know that cutting education is no way to move our country forward. We must do more, not less, to give Americans the tools they need to build a better life. Education is the key to everything we stand for as a nation.

WHY THE BEST
PLAN DIDN'T WIN:
A HEALTH-CARE QUIZ

❀❀❀❀❀❀❀❀❀❀❀❀

Home base for my political consulting business is an old town house where I've been for about seven years now. It's sort of small for an office, just a downstairs with some desks, a tiny kitchen, a really comfortable worn-in couch and an upstairs where my dogs hang out and I read my mail and gossip on the phone. The town house faces a tree-lined street with a little park at one end. It could be pretty much anywhere. Except just two blocks away, on the other end of the street—the nonpark end, as my dogs probably think of it—is the U.S. Capitol.

I've been watching policy making at close range for a while now. Washington sees its fair share of winners and losers, and from my front-row seat, I've noticed some pretty distinct patterns of postgame behavior.

The winners hold press conferences and rewrite their campaign brochures. You've seen it a thousand times—handshakes, bill signings, photo ops, and ceremonies where they serve canapés and glasses of chardonnay.

The losers deny responsibility and dole out blame. The press takes a lot of heat during this finger-pointing period. The logic goes something like this: If the media had done their job, the people would have gotten all the facts, and we wouldn't be standing here with our tails between our legs. Most of the time, this response is no more than grade A Washington baloney.

Except every once in a while, the press really doesn't do their job, and the people really don't get the facts, and a good plan can die a damn ugly death.

When the President and the First Lady set out to change health care in America, we knew they were in for a big fight. What we didn't know was that most of the press corps would do a lousy job of separating truth from fiction.

Despite a barrage of coverage, most Americans would still be hard-pressed to tell you much of what the Clinton health-care plan contained. Do you, for example, remember any specific provisions? How would health alliances have worked? What were the plan's cost-containment measures?

Unless you were one of the original drafters of the thing, I bet you're stumped. You're probably coming up short on information and long on images of waiting lines and mountains of red tape. Why? Well, you just didn't get the facts, and there's no reasonable way to expect you to know what was really in that plan.

But whose job was it to make sure that people understood this plan? Surely, most of the responsibility lay with the Administration—with the President and with his cabinet, his spokespeople, and his advisers like me. We took that responsibility seriously. We had briefings. Press conferences. Television commercials. Town hall meetings. Bus tours. Short of going door to door with free Band-Aids and Q-tips and a copy of our plan, we tried everything.

We never stood a chance.

The truth about the plan got lost in a gazillion-dollar tidal wave of Republican and special-interest propaganda; enterprising and truth-seeking news stories on the subject were few and far between.

. . .

Early on it seemed as if the Republicans understood that the country needed real reform. At a health-care summit in the Midwest, Bob Dole led a standing ovation for Hillary Rodham Clinton and announced, "We want to . . . establish that the Republicans are for real and want to help find a solution."[1]

But soon after, Republicans changed their tune. A major turning point came in December of 1993, when GOP guru Bill Kristol wrote a memorandum to Republican leaders making clear that a Clinton victory had to be avoided at all costs. Kristol argued that the administration's reform plan presented a "serious political threat," and he urged Republicans to adopt an "aggressive and uncompromising counterstrategy."[2]

Talk about a powerful memo.

Anyone who had been talking about working with the President pulled a quick about-face. In lockstep, the Republicans started reprimanding the Democrats for ever having uttered the words *health care* and *crisis* in the same breath. They said we needed a couple of minor changes instead of comprehensive reform. And eagerly taking their cues from Kristol, who warned the President's plan would lead to "rationing, queuing, diminished innovation, black markets, [and] the creation of a government 'health police,' " right-wingers turned on the propaganda machine.

Sen. Phil Gramm had some of the best lines. Remember this one? "When my momma gets sick, I want her to see a doctor, not a bureaucrat."[3] (Note to Phil Gramm: Your momma is able to see a doctor thanks to a program you want to slice up—Medicare). The Republicans' scare tactics got even more outrageous when they saw they could use health care as a way of raising money for their right-wing causes. In fund-raising letters, Phyllis Schlafly warned Americans, "Your health and freedom are in imminent danger of being taken over by the Federal Government. You will be prosecuted as a criminal if you try to buy better insurance or better care than what the bureaucrats in the Collective dictate."[4]

Not even a grain of truth in there, but bonus points to Schlafly for creativity.

So what's my point? I mean, Republicans lying about something President Clinton is for ain't exactly a news flash.

But this go-around, the press let them get away with murder.

When I first sat down to work on this book, I made a deal with myself: I would muster up every ounce of self-discipline I had and refrain from press bashing. But restraint ain't one of my more notable traits, and a little ways into the project, I decided I just couldn't address health care and not mention what a lousy, miserable, pathetic job the press did.

You won't catch me taking on the press corps single-handedly on this one. I have found me an unlikely ally: a member of the media itself. One night not too long ago I was watching TV, kind of dozing off, in lazy channel-surf mode. I paused briefly on C-SPAN and heard something that nearly made me fall off the damn couch. It was ABC anchor Peter Jennings, addressing a room full of media folks:

> On policy issues, we sometimes show a need to anoint or condemn. Prior to President Clinton's election, we did story after story on how messed up health care in the country was. Once he proposed his plan, we turned around and did stories on how change would do us so much harm, egged on, I might add, by the widest imaginable array of lobbyists.[5]

Mr. Jennings really hit the jackpot with that one.

And he isn't even the only journalist still ruminating about how bad the coverage was. Take columnist William Raspberry. He recently wrote, "During the debate over health care reform . . . it dawned on me that even as a fairly attentive consumer of news, I was never quite sure what was in any package or proposal. I knew only who seemed at the moment to be ahead on points, who was cheering for whom and what it all meant for Hillary's ascendancy or demise."[6]

Most reporters were unwilling to sift through lobbyists' lies to get to the heart of the matter. After all, it was so much easier and a lot more fun to write about fistfights on the Hill and the fortunes of the First Lady. You were far more likely to read about who was scoring political points at whose expense than about how the President's plan would affect you or how it compared with other plans for reform: In fact, in 1994 two out of three articles about health-care reform focused on political strategy and polling rather than substance.[7] It doesn't take a genius to figure out why many Americans just gave up in disgust and began to tune the whole thing out.

There were exceptions. Some reporters did bring hard work and objectivity to the task of figuring out not only the politics of the issue but the issue itself. Take Jim Fallows, the Washington editor of *The Atlantic Monthly*. Fallows patiently and skillfully blew each bit of conventional wisdom about the President's program to smithereens in an article about the plan's failure. The title of the article? "A Triumph of Misinformation."[8]

I couldn't have said it better myself.

When *The Wall Street Journal* and NBC conducted a poll in the middle of the whole debacle, people seemed pretty down on the "Clinton plan"; they thought it was "too confusing, too complex, and . . . too expensive." Then the pollsters read them a straight-up description of the President's bill—without telling them whose plan it was. Guess what? A whopping 76 percent of them liked what they heard.[9]

The Clinton plan failed not because there was a true debate on its merits; it failed because, in the end, it had been distorted beyond recognition.

So let's go back and peel away some of that misinformation and put some of those doubts to rest. Let's look at what was really in that plan, as well as what's going on today in health care. Because, my friends, this problem doesn't seem to be going away on its own. Health-care costs just keep going up. More and more working parents can't afford regular trips to the pediatrician for their kids, and every month 100,000 more folks lose their insurance. This is just too important to sweep under the rug.

I've designed a quiz about health-care reform for information-starved people like you—it takes into account that the media left you without much in the way of test prep. So in addition to some pretty bad cornball jokes, I've included lots of extra help—that's the stuff in italics. You know us fuzzy-headed, bleeding-heart liberals—we're always looking to give deserving folks a little extra help.

So sharpen up your No. 2 pencil and get going.

1. First things first. Do we need health-care reform in America?

   a. Heck no! We need fewer sick people.

   b. Well, maybe a little around the edges. But certainly nothing that might jeopardize generous PAC contributions from the insurance industry.

   c. We sure do. Something's not working right when we've got 43 million folks out there without insurance and skyrocketing health-care costs.

   ☞ *We've got some damn fine medical care available in our country—cutting-edge technology, amazing research institutions, and lots of doctors and nurses who are dedicated to what they do. But the price of insurance just keeps going up—both for individuals and for small businesses. Too many hardworking Americans are without insurance, and too many others are just one pink slip or job switch away from losing theirs. Medical bills from an ordinary illness can bankrupt a middle-class family without coverage. Insurance companies pick the people they want to cover, seeking out the healthiest Americans, so they rake in big bucks and can afford to contribute to defeating any reform plan that might change the status quo.*

2. The President's Health Security Act set out a game plan for extending coverage to millions of uninsured families, controlling health-care costs, and reducing paperwork and bureaucracy. How would this have worked? Well, through universal coverage, managed competition, employer mandates, and health alliances. Uh-oh, you're thinking. That's where I ran into trouble the last time around. But just give these definitions a shot:

A. Universal Coverage:

a. What you have when your lobbyists have gotten to every important congressional committee member.

b. A giant socialist government takeover plot!

c. Comprehensive health benefits for all Americans that can never be taken away. The right thing *and* the smart thing to do.

☞ *You know why universal coverage is the right thing to do. Here's a hint on why it might be the smart thing to do. Number one: Although it seems to cut against common sense, the more folks who have coverage, the less costs go up. For insurance to work efficiently, you've got to spread the risk among as many people as possible. Number two: Today, people without insurance hold off on getting treated until the last possible minute, when their conditions have become full-blown; then they show up in the emergency room. Emergency care is unbelievably expensive; preventive care and early treatment make a lot more sense.*

B. Managed Competition:

a. A gentleman's agreement between Phil Gramm and Bob Dole to refrain from slinging "your momma" insults at each other during televised debates.

b. A giant socialist government takeover plot!

c. A market-based reform in which groups of doctors or hospitals compete for patients.

☞ *Managed competition would mean your boss would have to give you a choice of plans, so that you'd be the one who decides what's right for you and your family. You'd receive "report cards" on available health plans, so it would be easy to compare plans and figure out what you needed. Like the idea of more control? That's what you'd have, with lower premiums to boot. And despite the grim message from GOP fear-mongers, you would* always *have had the option of staying with your own doctor. Let me repeat that for those of you who saw too many damn commercials and are hard of hearing on the subject: Under Clinton's health-care plan, you would* always *have been able to keep your own doctor.*

C. *Employer Mandate:*

a. What your boss claims to have when he gives your parking space to his Uncle Morty.

b. A giant socialist government takeover plot!

c. Employers are responsible for paying a portion of their employees' insurance premium. A mandate built on our existing system, in which more than eight out of ten people with insurance are covered through their employers.[10]

☞ *Republicans claimed that small businesses would have been devastated by reform, but the fact is, the Clinton plan would have ensured that small businesses got the same deal that big businesses get today. Many small businesses already offer their workers insurance, but doing so isn't easy. Small firms pay much higher premiums than large companies, and while their coverage costs more, it often offers less. Listen to* The Wall Street Journal *on the subject: "For many small businesses, saddled with escalating health care costs, President Clinton's health care package comes as an unexpected windfall.*"[11]

D. *Health Alliance:*

a. A little-known group of cartoon superheroes who encourage children to eat whole-wheat bread and veggies.

b. A giant socialist government takeover plot!

c. Small businesses and individual consumers band together to negotiate for high-quality health care at an affordable price. These alliances would have the same bargaining heft that big companies enjoy today.

☞ *Here's how the insurance system works today: Picture hundreds of thousands of businesses negotiating with thousands of insurance companies for coverage for their employees. Under the President's plan, health alliances would do the hard work, cutting through the red tape and driving down administrative costs for businesses and individuals.*

3. Hawaii is the only state in America that requires its employers to contribute to the cost of their employees' health care, as the Clinton plan would have done. The results?

a. Hula injuries are down 10 percent thanks to increased preventive care.

b. Total devastation! Thousands are fleeing! A second Pearl Harbor!

c. Nearly everyone is covered—something no other state can say. And don't forget lower costs: Universal coverage has meant more primary care and fewer hospital and emergency room visits.

4. Special-interest groups with giant financial stakes in the status quo felt threatened by reform and spent lots of money to misrepresent the President's plan. How much did these lobbyists spend?

a. Hundreds of millions, plus $50 for marriage counseling to keep Harry and Louise together. How bad was their marriage? All they ever talked about was health care. Harry, she's a good-looking woman in her sexual prime. Get a clue.

b. So what if hundreds of millions were spent? A small price to pay to defeat a giant socialist government takeover plot!

c. Well, now, what do you want to include? Merely the hundreds of millions spent on attack advertising? Or in addition, the $79 million given to congressional candidates by opponents of the President's plan?[12]

☞ *These are big numbers we're talking now—in fact, the country has never seen such an expensive lobbying effort.[13] Given how much these special interests spent, we desperately needed fair press coverage to cut through the bull. So much for that.*

5. Republican distortions concerning health care are not exactly a brand-new phenomenon. Medicare is the federal health insurance program that pays for doctors' fees, hospital stays, and home health care for the elderly and the disabled. When Democrats fought to enact Medicare in 1965, congressional Republicans came up with every possible excuse to oppose it, and the GOP rhetoric of that time is all too familiar today. Which of the following distortions do you personally find the most odious?

a. Republican Representative James Utt: "Let us not go on the assumption here that we are not destroying the quality and quantity of medicine and that we are not socializing medicine, because that is exactly what we are doing."[14]

b. Republican Sen. Roman Hruska charged: "With Federal funds comes Federal control. In the area of medical care, Federal interference presents frightening prospects."[15]

c. Republican House Leader and future President Gerald Ford (MI): "We are going to find our aged bewildered by a multi-headed bureaucratic maze of confusion over what program covers what and who is on first base."[16]

☞ *It's a good thing the Republicans lost their battle against Medicare. Because before Medicare was enacted, more than half of the seniors in this country had no health insurance and many of those who did were underinsured. Today, more than 37 million Americans—including 99 percent of our senior citizens—are protected by Medicare. And what about their doom and gloom predictions of a confusing, bureaucratic mess? As it turns out, Medicare spends a whole lot less on overhead than private plans. And seniors report that they are happier with their health insurance than are privately insured patients.*[17]

6. Thirty years after they fought the enactment of Medicare tooth and nail, Republicans now tell the American people that the survival of the program hinges on the GOP plan to slash $270 billion in funding. And because Republicans just go nuts when Democrats suggest there is a link between GOP tax breaks for the rich and GOP Medicare proposals, why don't we go ahead and take their plan at face value? That's right, assume it's a mere coincidence that they proposed cutting $245 billion in taxes at the same time they proposed $270 billion in Medicare cuts. Just what would their proposal accomplish?

a. Screw that proposal. I've got a better idea. Pay this year's Medicare bills with the Discover card. Maybe we'd get 1 percent back.

b. Sure this proposal would mean an end to ensuring equality of access and care for all elderly Americans. But it's about time. After all, the more money you made before your retirement, the better care you should receive in your golden years.

c. The Republican plan offers seniors three options: stay in the current system (but face higher premiums), join a managed care plan (but face more restrictions), or start a Medical Savings Account (not a great idea unless you're healthy and wealthy). Bottom line: No good news for poor or middle-income folks. The rich will come out ahead in benefits, amount of care, and ability to choose their doctor.[18]

☞ *The Republicans have opposed Medicare for thirty years, and now we're supposed to believe that their $270 billion cut is a well-intended effort to save Medicare? The New York Times doesn't: "The cuts being pushed through Congress . . . threaten to dry up money for medical training, devastate nursing homes and drive hospitals and doctors away from taking care of Medicare patients . . . health programs for the elderly are bearing a disproportionate share of the austerity being pushed by the Republicans."[19]*

You'd think they would find this embarrassing. But they don't; they just keep parroting their lines about protecting Medicare. Except every once in a while, they let down their guard and show their real feelings. Listen to the leaders of the GOP just this last October.

Sen. Bob Dole: "I was there, fighting the fight, voting against Medicare—one of twelve—because we knew it wouldn't work in 1965."[20]

And his buddy Newt Gingrich: "Now, we didn't get rid of it [Medicare] in round one because we don't think that's politically smart and we don't think that's the right way to go through a transition. But we believe it's going to wither on the vine."[21]

Who honestly believes that these guys are out there trying to save Medicare?

I mean, who could be naive enough to believe their outrageous distortions? Apparently the Republicans think our senior citizens are. In a memorandum entitled "Everything You Ever Wanted to Know about Communicating Medicare," the GOP pollster Frank Luntz advised Republicans to keep in mind that older Americans are "pack-oriented" and "susceptible to following one very dominant person's lead."[22]

I guess I never introduced Frank to Miss Nippy.

7. Medicaid is the other major federal health insurance program. Which of the following groups receives the largest chunk of Medicaid funds?

a. Medicaid? You mean Medic Aid? Like when all those rock stars put on a concert to raise money for doctors?

b. Able-bodied poor people, you know, all those folks who collect a welfare check (read: minorities).

c. The elderly, the blind, and the disabled.

☞ *Look. I'm just going to give this one away. People are always thinking that Medicaid is only for poor, inner-city folks. That's just not so. Nearly two-thirds of Medicaid funds are spent on Americans who are elderly, blind, or disabled. Medicaid provides health insurance for more than 30 million people, and deep cuts in the program will leave many—as many as 8 million—without any coverage whatsoever. And if the program that supports two out of three patients in nursing homes is decimated, who's going to foot the bill? You got it. Middle-class Americans are going to have to come up with some serious extra money each year to make sure their parents get the care they need. That's not where the problems with long-term care end either: Republicans would like to eliminate federal enforcement of nursing-home standards, which Ronald Reagan signed into law. The laws were enacted to protect seniors from the unsafe and unsanitary conditions that had been found in many of America's institutions. Here's another example of Republicans doing something shortsighted and inane because they think that federal regulations are all that stand between us and Nirvana.*

Well, if you've made it this far, I thank you for your patience and fortitude. I'd give you an answer key but I imagine that you got enough hints along the way to make grading yourself a pretty straightforward affair.

I realize this exam may have convinced you that I'm some kinda gloom-and-doom partisan. Some guy who is pissed off that his party lost Congress. And, you know, I'd be willing to give Republicans the benefit of the doubt and assume that they were truly concerned with the health and well-being of Americans. But that wouldn't explain the fact that they tried to shelve meat inspection regulations, or that they've proposed lowering FDA approval standards (the United States has the best record for preventing unsafe drugs from reaching consumers), or that they want to remove air quality regulations and repeal clean water standards.

And it wouldn't explain why the Republicans in Congress have passed zero, zip, nothing to reform health care this year (don't you dare count their proposals to slash Medicare and Medicaid by almost half a trillion dollars)—although after defeating the President's health-care plan, Sen. Dole claimed that legislation addressing the cost and quality of health care would be "at the top of the Senate agenda" this year.[23]

Don't hold your breath. The Republicans are better at shooting plans down than they are at offering solutions to the problems of rising health-care costs and increasing insecurity. But there's no sense in us Democrats giving up hope. There's a lot of work out there left to be done. We've got to keep trying to reform the insurance market to help out American families. And we must work to fix what's wrong with Medicare and Medicaid but also to preserve what is right, never forgetting how many people are protected by these programs.

Now before I wrap this up, I have a confession to make. I've been telling you that rabid Republicans, profligate special interests, and a pathetic press corps killed the administration's sensible plan to reform health care. Completely true—but I'm leaving something out.

The President's plan was very much a market-oriented plan, but the federal government was also a part of the picture—and it would have played an important role in increasing access and reducing costs. Too many of us Democrats bought into the right-wing notion that government is synonymous with failure. At a time when Americans are being encouraged to lose faith in the ability of their government to do good, we shied away from explaining how the government could play a legitimate role in reform. Our reluctance to do this made it easier—not harder—for the bad guys to misrepresent the plan.

There's a good lesson in that. We can't just sit on our butts and hope that the next time we introduce a good plan for health-care reform Americans will somehow have regained their faith in the federal government. It just won't work that way. We've got to make the case ourselves, and we've got to do it with conviction.

A (Too) Brief Note
on Why I'm Discouraged
About Race

❀ ❀ ❀ ❀ ❀ ❀ ❀

The subject of race is something I have lived with and thought about my entire life. In all candor I resisted addressing the subject of race in this book because it has become extremely difficult to discuss. More than that, it's difficult to see a happy ending in the near future, and God knows we progressives need some happy endings these days. But you can't talk about what's right and wrong with this country without dealing with race.

In matters of race, I would probably fit the classic definition of a white liberal. I am an integrationist. Remember those? I believe in the positive value of people of different colors having a lot to do with one another.

This point of view has taken some hard blows. I had hoped by now we would be moving toward one America, yet, frankly, it appears that the country is hardening in its prejudices. This was brought home to me by two recent events, public reaction to the verdict in the O. J. Simpson case and Louis Farrakhan's Million Man March.

I had what I imagine was the typical white liberal take on the Simpson trial: They framed a guilty man. But what really moved me was not what happened inside that courtroom, but what happened outside. I will never forget the news footage of reactions around the nation to the not-guilty verdict. College auditoriums with wildly cheering black students, restaurants with ecstatic black diners, offices with relieved and happy black employees. It is difficult to come to terms with the level of anger and disgust so many black people—rich, poor, and in-between (where you live and what you do didn't seem to be the issue)—clearly have for the country's criminal justice system. It is so stunningly obvious that we do, in fact, see the world through two different lenses.

Strong leadership and hard work can move this country toward a day when we don't live in such different worlds.

Which is why I find the widespread acceptance and enthusiastic support for Louis Farrakhan so disturbing. Look, I'm sure there were a lot of complicated reasons for black men to show up in Washington for the Million Man March last October, and I'm not attacking the people who attended, plenty of whom were responding to the message of self-reliance, self-determination, pride, and the value of the family. But Farrakhan is a bigot, filled with hate and venom. This guy is a splinter figure looking for some action, not a leader ready and able to make a difference.

Suppose you had asked me at the 1963 civil rights March on Washington—a march dominated by the vision of Dr. Martin Luther King, Jr.—where I thought the country was going to be in terms of race relations thirty years later. I would have said, "We'll have made a lot of progress." Now, race relations *have* improved since 1963. But we're nowhere close to what we dreamed of. For one thing, instead of Dr. King's "I Have a Dream" speech, we've got Louis Farrakhan spreading hate and spewing some goofy numerology about the height of the Washington Monument. That's no way to plan for a better America. Going from Dr. King to Louis Farrakhan ain't progress, it's regress.

We're losing this game. I mean, you'd have to be blind not to see that the American dream of racial harmony and equal opportunity is a long, long way off. People don't even seem to agree that these should be our goals! Too many white people say, "Look, we've had these programs and we've done our part and that's it, to hell with them." And too many black people say, "We've always been victims of racism and we continue to be victims of racism, to hell with them." It's a very destructive place for our country to be—one where there doesn't seem to be too much room for brotherhood and common ground.

There's no law you can pass to eliminate hatred if it's in people's hearts, but you can make harmony a national goal. The President gave a speech in Austin on the day of the Farrakhan march that was 100 percent on the mark. He said, "We must clean our house. There are too many today, white and black, on the left and right, on the street corners and the radio waves, who seek to sow division for their own purposes. To them I say: No more. We must be one. Here in 1995, on the edge of the 21st century, we dare not tolerate the existence of two Americas."[1]

You don't hear too many speeches like that from our leaders anymore. In fact, you don't see too many politicians using their public office to move us forward on race matters. This is especially true in the South, where Zell Miller of Georgia and Jim Hunt of North Carolina are lonely exceptions. When I was growing up, Earl Long risked his entire political career and ultimately his sanity by refusing to engage in race baiting. Now my native state of Louisiana has as governor Mike Foster, a man who doesn't repudiate the support of David Duke, an American Nazi. North Carolina's senior senator is Jesse Helms, and there's nothing in this man's record to indicate that he believes in racial harmony and everything in his record to indicate that he promotes racial discord.

The Contract with America is a direct assault on black people. Period. From decimating the earned income tax credit to cuts in education and job training, the entire thing is an attack. And at a time when we're sliding in the wrong direction, it looks like the Republicans are saying, "Well, rather than slide, let's just turn around and run." It looks like they are washing their hands of all responsibility for anybody but well-to-do white folks.

SEE HOW THEY USE RACE

This stuff doesn't require me to spin—not even a quarter turn. Here it is, straight up:

- **Ronald Reagan and States' Rights**
  - In 1980, Ronald Reagan kicked off his general-election campaign with a speech at the Nashoba County Fair in Philadelphia, Mississippi, in which he endorsed states' rights.[*] An interesting topic to bring up: "States' rights" was the battle cry of those who opposed desegregation in the 1960s. And an even more interesting choice of location: In the summer of 1964, three young civil rights workers were murdered in Nashoba County, Mississippi.

- **Lamar Smith and Midnight Basketball**
  - Lamar Smith, a Republican who represents the 21st Congressional District in Texas, said that midnight basketball, a recreational program for inner-city kids, is "based on the theory that the person who stole your car, robbed your house and assaulted your family is no more than a would-be NBA star."[†]

- **Jesse Helms: Thanks for the Nomination**
  - While a guest on *Larry King Live* this past September, Senator Jesse Helms took a call from Tilk, Alabama:

    "I think that you should get a Nobel Peace Prize for everything you've done to help keep down the niggers," the caller said.

    "Thank you, I think," Helms replied.[‡]

---

[*] Martin Schram, "Carter Says Reagan Injects Racism," *Washington Post*, Sept. 17, 1980.

[†] Elizabeth Shogren, "Midnight Basketball Is Winner on Street," *Los Angeles Times*, Aug. 19, 1994.

[‡] John Monk, "Helms Reply to Slur Criticized," *Houston Chronicle*, Sept. 14, 1995.

It's one thing to encourage self-reliance, and quite another to propose that the government has no responsibility for the poor, no responsibility for the victims of discrimination. Republicans want to get rid of affirmative action and return America to a meritocracy, but America has never been a real meritocracy. There has always been racism, and to eliminate affirmative action is to return the country to a past when jobs were controlled by whites and given mostly to whites.

The question you get from a lot of white America is, Why should we care? And it comes down to this: We are all Americans. No one I know understands this better than the President, who told his audience in Austin, "We must be one as neighbors, as fellow citizens, not separate camps, but families—white, black . . . all of us, no matter how different, who share basic American values and are willing to live by them. When a child is gunned down on a street in the Bronx, no matter what our race, he is our American child. Whether we like it or not, we are one nation, one family, indivisible, and for us, divorce or separation are not options."[2]

America is supposed to be a country whose essential promise is based on opportunity. Most immigrants came to the United States for opportunity for themselves. But let's face it, blacks originally came to this country to provide opportunity for planters who wanted to make more money. And the truth is that for a lot of blacks today, their greatest opportunities are to be harassed by a cop, to be redlined by a mortgage company, to go hungry when they're young, to attend inferior schools, and to get thrown in prison. Not exactly the kind of opportunity America is supposed to be built on.

CONCLUSION:
IT'S UP TO US

✸ ✸ ✸ ✸ ✸ ✸ ✸

Two years ago, I was selected to receive an honorary doctorate and give the commencement speech at Louisiana State University, my alma mater. It was a huge honor and quite a turn of affairs. I mean, I didn't exactly distinguish myself academically when I was a student there. I racked up fifty-six hours of F's—including three in golf—before I flunked out. I eventually finished my degree after getting some discipline and good sense beaten into me in the Marine Corps, but no one would have mistaken me for a scholar, even after I returned. The best you could say is that I was a lousy student who, with the help of some masochistic perseverance and down-home wisdom, eventually managed to make good.

When I got up to give my speech that day at LSU, I looked out at that huge audience and saw my whole family: Miss Nippy; my wife, Mary; my seven brothers and sisters, their spouses and kids. I saw my high school and college buddies. I saw my doctor, teachers, even the lady from the Bookmobile. Everyone but my daddy, who passed away a decade and a half too early to witness this near-unthinkable event.

After a minute of waves and thank-yous, I reached into the inside pocket of my blazer and—dammit! I had forgotten my speech back at the hotel. I looked down at Mary, and she knew immediately what had happened. But what could I do? I just had to wing it.

So I rambled on for a little while about what an honor this all was and about all the memories it brought back. I got some nods and applause, but I knew I wasn't giving those graduating seniors what they wanted to hear most.

I knew they didn't expect a fancy message with all kinds of literary allusions and historical mumbo jumbo. But what did they want? Well, I figured it was pretty simple: They were just looking for their commencement speaker to launch them off into the real world with a head of steam and a rush of optimism.

That's exactly what I tried to give them: "Look, my friends, if a guy with my grades can get an honorary doctorate and a guy with my looks can marry a woman as wonderful as Mary Matalin, there's great hope for all the rest of you stupid and ugly folks!"

The students loved it. And not just the stupid and ugly ones.

The reason I bring up this little story is that I want to send all of you folks off into the real world of backyard barbecues and school board meetings with an equally straightforward message of optimism. But I'm no fool, I know I've got a much harder task here. I'm looking out at you in bookland, and instead of seeing a bunch of wide-eyed kids who are proud of their accomplishments and champing at the bit to confront the challenges ahead, I'm seeing a mass of tired-looking Democrats with long faces and slumped shoulders.

This is a very tough time. Not just because we are in the minority in Congress; it's more fundamental than that. Every single one of our core beliefs is under relentless assault. Who would have predicted we'd have to defend the idea that the federal government of the richest nation on earth should be holding up a modest safety net for its most vulnerable citizens? Or that in a time of sacrifice the wealthiest interests should be expected to pony up like everyone else? Or even that the government should be in the business of supporting public education? These are not crazy, outlandish ideas. A few years ago, they were beyond question. Yet now we're back on our heels, off balance, not knowing what they're going to hit us with next.

The Republicans are getting pretty cocky. Throughout Washington and around the country, right-wingers are already popping corks and toasting the demise of the liberal ideology. William Bennett, the former Secretary of Education, has predicted that "under Bill Clinton's watch . . . we may see the end of liberalism in our time."[1] Bill Kristol, the Republican strategist, would have you believe that liberalism is due to follow communism into the scrap heap of history: "Liberalism is like a huge, condemned building. It is big and impressive, but one well-placed charge could bring down the whole edifice. The world saw this happen in Eastern Europe and the former Soviet Union in the 1980s."[2]

Hey, I wish I could tell you that these guys are completely off the mark. I really do. But the truth of the matter is that they could be right. The way things are going, liberalism may not be long for this world.

But make no mistake: If liberalism disappears, it will not be because right-wing Republicans have set charges under our building. If anything, the right-wingers have given us the steel girders and support beams we need to shore everything up.

Think about it. Reasonable, clear-thinking Republicans have lost the war of priorities to a band of extremists in their own party. No longer do we have to make slippery-slope arguments about what *might* happen if the most intolerant, greedy, and shortsighted elements take over the Republican Party. It's happened. Newt Gingrich, until recently a zealot backbencher, is the Speaker of the House of Representatives. Jesse Helms, the man who once warned President Clinton that he "better have a bodyguard" if he tried to set foot on a military base in North Carolina, writes the Senate's foreign relations policy. Rush Limbaugh is the party's loudest spokesman. Pat Robertson and his Christian Coalition are its most powerful interest group. As we saw in Houston in '92, these people can make our case in ways that we never could by ourselves.

So, if progressivism folds we will not have any right to go pointing fingers at the Republican Party. And we sure as hell won't go pointing fingers at the voters. We will have only ourselves to blame. It will be our fault, and ours alone. It will mean that we were mute when we should have been defending what we believe.

Have you ever heard the story of the old lady from New Orleans and her amazing parrot? The bird was a fabulous creature. It was always gentle and polite, and you've never seen such brilliant colors in your life. But the most impressive thing about that parrot was the way it could speak. I'm not talking about squawking out a few *Polly want a crackers*. The old lady had taught that parrot to speak in perfect sentences. And not just in one language, mind you. The parrot spoke five languages fluently!

Seeing as the bird was sort of like the child she never had, the southern lady hated to leave it all alone in an empty house. So one day when she had to take a drive around town, she got the dim-witted Cajun boy from down the street to come in and watch it.

Big mistake. The boy got hungry, and he plopped the parrot into a big pot of gumbo.

When the lady arrived home, she saw the boy eating the bird and went crazy. "How could you do this? That was the most incredible bird on the planet! That bird could speak five languages!"

The boy was sad and confused at the same time. "Of them five languages, was English one uh them?" he asked.

"Well, of course it was," the lady said, consumed with tears.

"Then why," asked the boy, "didn't he just say somethin'?"

Wake up, people! If we progressives don't speak up in our own behalf in a language everyone can understand, how can we expect to survive? It shouldn't take a dim-witted Cajun boy to point this out. It's just common sense.

. . .

But if we're going to get serious about defending ourselves, where do we start?

The first step is to get busy reminding people what we've accomplished and what kind of place we'd be living in now if we Democrats and we liberals had not played such a huge role in setting the course of this nation.

Up until now we've been foolish enough to leave our history to a pseudohistorian like Newt Gingrich. No more. It's our turn to prove to America that there has never been a political party or a political philosophy in this or any other country that has achieved as much as ours. And we don't need to turn back to the early days of our party under Thomas Jefferson in order to make that case. We can focus on the precise period—the past six decades—which the Republicans are most keen on distorting beyond all recognition.

The dawn of that era was, of course, Franklin Delano Roosevelt's New Deal. Funny thing happens when the Republicans talk about that turning point in this nation's history. On the one hand, they will gladly tell you that their primary mission in life is to tear down FDR's New Deal legacy. On the other hand, many right-wingers just can't resist trying to wrap themselves in the mantle of FDR. Newt Gingrich even had the audacity to say that if Roosevelt were alive today, he would be a wholehearted supporter of the Contract with America![3]

Let's play compare and contrast. After the original Hundred Days, when FDR brought this country back from the edge of social and financial collapse in the Great Depression, this nation became, in the words of the journalist Walter Lippmann, "an organized nation confident of our power . . . to control our own destiny."[4] After Gingrich's "Hundred Days," we are confident only of our power to afflict the afflicted and comfort the comfortable. FDR told the nation that "the test of our progress is not whether we add more to the abundance of those who have much; it is whether we provide enough for those who have little."[5] Newt tells the nation that the test of our progress is whether we can cut enough money from Medicare and school lunches, and get rid of AmeriCorps and the Department of Education. FDR is the reason our senior citizens have Social Security, our unemployed workers can count on some help in getting back on their feet, our families have guaranteed bank deposits, our veterans have a G.I. Bill to help with their schooling, and our investors can buy stock without worrying about getting swindled. Newt Gingrich is the reason we may lose the safety net under our children. I didn't know FDR, but this I can say with utter authority: Newt, you are no FDR!

FDR's successor, Harry S Truman, is another liberal Democrat whose image the Republicans love to steal for their own use. Let's take Truman's image back and start showing some pride in what he accomplished. We've got a lot to brag about. It was Truman, the Democrat, who had the foresight to sign the Marshall Plan and rebuild Western Europe. Truman, the Democrat, delivered the first civil rights message to Congress and signed the executive order to desegregate the armed forces. Truman, the Democrat, called for expanding Social Security, increasing federal help for education, raising the minimum wage, and launching a national health insurance program.

We should look back with nothing but satisfaction at all the things this party and this philosophy accomplished during the next forty years, the period of uninterrupted Democratic control of the House. The Democrats helped bring down Jim Crow with the Civil Rights Act of 1964 and the Voting Rights Act of 1965, maybe the two most significant pieces of legislation this century. We are still waiting for the Republicans to do something—anything—to bridge the racial divide in this country. (And, no, putting Clarence Thomas on the Supreme Court doesn't count!)

The Democrats were the champions of federal support for disadvantaged schools, which greatly increased the number of black

TEN THINGS YOU CAN DO

Civic duty is far from dull these days. There's a lot going on out there when it comes to politics and policy. You've got to make your voice heard. The best way, of course, is to vote—and I mean in every election, from the race for dogcatcher all the way up. But voting is not enough. Good Democrats need to roll up their sleeves and jump into the mix in many other ways, too.

Here is a simple list of ways you can make a difference:

1. Run for office.

It may seem old-fashioned, but I still believe that good people can do great things from elected office. And I'm not just trying to drum up business; you don't need some overpriced consultant to run your race. Put together a platform you believe in and go for it.

2. Volunteer on a campaign.

If you don't want to run for office, volunteer for someone who does. It can be in a local campaign or in the local branch of a national campaign. Campaigns are always short on money, and volunteers are the heart and soul of most efforts.

3. Talk to your children about public affairs and politics.

Make sure your dinner-table talk goes beyond Power Rangers and the prom. There's an old saying: "War is too important to be left to the generals." Civic discussions are too important to be left to television talking heads.

4. Write letters to the editor.

Give newspaper readers a chance to read something more intelligent and insightful than the normal editorial goop.

5. Go to town hall meetings.

Scandalously few people actually show up at these. Call up your county commissioner, your state representative, your city councilperson. Find out where and when you can go to speak your mind, or to just listen.

6. Attend school board meetings.

Even if you don't have kids in your local school system, you better believe that what goes on in those schools affects you.

7. Write members of Congress.

In these days of phony-baloney Astroturf lobbying, real letters from real people count.

8. Write a check.

Sit down with your family, decide how much you can afford to give, and get it out there to a candidate or cause you admire. Don't be afraid to send a note with the money.

9. Get involved in discussions on the Internet.

I'm serious. Although I personally have a better chance of flying a 747 than I do of finding the on-off switch on my office computer, I hear the Internet is a great way to get involved and stay informed.

Here's a quick list of ways you can find good Dems in cyberspace:

• Check out these Web sites: The White House (http://www.white-house.gov), Digital Democrats (http://www.webcom.com/~digitals), Democratic National Committee (http://www.democrats.org), Democratic Leadership Council (http://www.dlcppi.org/heads.htm).

• Subscribe to *The Internet Democrat*, a free E-mail newsletter; send the message "subscribe" (no quotes) to internet-democrats-request@webcom.com.

• Subscribe to the Demtalk list server; send the message "subscribe" (no quotes) to Demtalk-list@aquilapub.clever.net.

10. Be just as willing to compliment as you are to criticize.

The last thing we need is more cynicism. Be constructive.

children graduating from high school. Democrats created Head Start, and as Congressman Robert Torricelli (D-NJ) put it in an op-ed piece about a year ago, it "remains the single most successful program ever devised for maintaining high-risk children in school."[6]

The Democrats couldn't stand to see kids go to bed hungry. They set up a winner of a program called WIC to help pregnant mothers and infants get the food and medicine they need, lowering infant mortality and health-care costs at the same time. They increased the money for our schools to serve free breakfasts and lunches to those who need them. Under Presidents Kennedy and Johnson, they took a spotty food stamp program and turned it into a nutritional safety net. All in all, when we had the political will to help poor kids, back in the 1960s, we cut the rate of childhood poverty almost in half. And we did it because that was the right thing to do.

As I've said a number of times before in this book, the Democrats also cut the rate of elderly poverty in half. But unlike childhood poverty, which spiked up again in the 1980s, elderly poverty has stayed nice and low. The main reason: Social Security, a program the Democrats created, expanded, and defended against repeated raids.

The Democrats in Congress also gave our senior citizens a huge quality-of-life boost in the form of Medicare and Medicaid. In 1965, when LBJ signed both plans into law, more than half the people over sixty-five had no health insurance at all. Now almost everyone is covered, and, as LBJ predicted, "older citizens . . . no longer have to fear that illness will wipe out their savings, eat up their income, and destroy lifelong hope of dignity and independence."[7]

We can't forget, either, that having the Democrats in control of Congress saved the environment from devastation. It was the Democrats who came up with the radical idea that the country would be better off if industries didn't dump whatever the hell they wanted into our lakes and rivers—then passed the Clean Water Act. The Democrats banned all kinds of pesticides and other chemicals that were killing off our birds and fish. They dragged the Republicans and the auto industry kicking and screaming into the Energy Policy and Conservation Act of 1975, which scored us a 100 percent gain in gas efficiency.[8] And they made huge progress in cleaning up our air. Since 1970, when Congress passed the first Clean Air Act, the U.S. economy has expanded by more than 85 percent, the population has grown by 28 percent, and vehicle travel has more than doubled. Air pollution, thanks to a healthy set of Democratic priorities, has *dropped* by a quarter.[9] The Democrats did that.

And don't think for a minute that we're going to shortchange President Clinton when we get to reeling off our accomplishments! Look at education. The President streamlined our school loans, created a new national service corps, provided school-to-work opportunities for kids who aren't going on to college, increased funding for Head Start, and raised educational standards around the country with Goals 2000.

President Clinton pushed through the Brady Bill, requiring a five-day waiting period for handgun purchases, and a year later he gave Americans a historic $30 billion crime bill, complete with a ban on the deadliest assault weapons and a provision to add 100,000 cops to the beat. He signed the Family and Medical Leave Act, which does a whole lot more to promote "family values" than anything we've seen from the current Republican Congress. By expanding the earned income tax credit, he cut taxes on 15 million working Americans and helped make work pay.

And how easy it is to forget that the President proposed and fought for the largest deficit-cutting plan in history. George Bush's deficit ran up to $290 billion. When Bill Clinton took office, Congress was predicting that we'd now be running a deficit of $310 billion a year. But, thanks to the President's efforts and strong economic growth, the deficit has been cut nearly in half.

Again, if it weren't for the interest we're paying on all the debt Reagan and Bush ran up, we'd have no deficit at all.

Deficit reduction is not the only reason we should be proud of that economic plan. Right before the President signed the plan, Phil Gramm, a former economics professor and, as of this writing, presidential candidate, made the cocksure prediction that "hundreds of thousands of Americans will lose their jobs because of this bill."[10] Right after it passed, he said, "We are buying a one-way ticket to a recession."[11]

Au contraire, mon frère. Thanks in part to that plan, the economy couldn't be stronger, and we're adding jobs at a record pace. In fact, job growth under President Clinton has been better than under any Republican administration since the 1920s.

To steal from Vice President Gore, everything that's supposed to be down is down, and everything that's supposed to be up is up. Unemployment is down, business investment is up. Inflation is down, productivity is up. Mortgage rates are down, new business starts are up. The misery index is down to its lowest point in more than twenty-five years. And the stock market has been going up like gangbusters.

We still have a long way to go in terms of making sure that everyone's getting a piece of all these economic gains, but any way you look at it, this President has made Gramm's economics look as goofy as Gingrich's history.

You feeling fired up yet? I hope so, because the next step is harder than the last. This is where we focus on the big picture. There is no question that a whole lot of good can come of talking about specific battles and specific victories, but now it's time for laying down general principles.

In the good old days, people knew full well what it meant to be a progressive or a liberal. They also knew full well what it meant to be a Democrat. Of course, we've always had a big tent with people holding up a hundred different banners. But the fact is, we had a good, solid, waterproof tent. Even when we were arguing inside the tent, we felt safe and protected from the harsh elements outside.

Not anymore. Now our tent's leaking, and the thunderstorm outside is pouring in. Some of us are wet and cold and shivering in the corner. Some of us are running off in search of fairer weather or a sturdier tent.

So what do we do about it? Well, my friends, we're going to patch up our tent. The only real way to do that is by making it a whole lot clearer to everyone what we stand for and where we want to take the country.

I hope this book is a start. In each chapter I've tried to give you more than just quick rebuttals. I've tried to give you a good look at what I call the 5/65 principles:

1. Promoting work and training for work should be the first domestic priority of government.

2. There is no way that the benefits of cutting taxes on the rich are going to trickle down to those in the middle and at the bottom. It just doesn't work!

3. The real answer to our social problems is, like the parable says, giving out fishing lessons; it is not, like the Republicans say, draining the pond.

4. The concept of progressive taxation—the idea that those who make more money pay a larger share of their income in taxes—is nonnegotiable.

5. Reinventing the outdated and inefficient parts of our federal government is responsible. Reversing its major successes—the cleanup of the environment, the protection of our food and drugs, the reduction in elderly poverty—is shameful.

6. This nation can't move forward when a majority of its citizens are getting left behind.

7. We must make public education work, and we know how to do it—not by using tax dollars for private schools but by setting higher goals and then helping our kids reach them.

8. Our health-care system is hurting; no one's going to cure it by cutting the heart out of the care we give our senior citizens and disabled kids.

9. Stable, two-parent families, while not always possible, are almost always preferable.

10. The fate of our party and our philosophy rests in our hands. If the public loses faith in us, we have no one to blame but ourselves.

This is a distilled list. There are plenty more nonnegotiable principles that I didn't touch on nearly enough. But, you know, we don't need to complicate matters. When I'm traveling around the country, a lot of people tell me that they think the debates in Washington are already too damned complicated. God knows, it's not because the folks in Congress are geniuses. It's just that after a while everything turns into a blur of numbers and programs and committee votes and last-minute deals and special interests and talking heads. Who can follow it all? Politicians can't even agree on whether something is a cut or not. How can most Americans hope to figure out what's really happening?

Well, it's no mystery what's going on right now in our nation's capital. It's actually quite simple. If you can somehow screen out the day-to-day theatrics, you're left with an age-old clash of visions. The contrasts are as clear and basic as can be.

Democrats believe that we are stronger united than divided. Republicans believe that unity is all well and good, unless of course that means having to share their communities with people who don't think like them, look like them, or act like them.

Democrats believe that a fortunate person ought to be willing to pay a little more so someone else will have an extra opportunity in life. Republicans believe that asking more from the fortunate is "socialist redistribution."

Democrats believe that while the market is by far the best economic system ever devised, it isn't always going to give us safe drugs, foods, workplaces, and consumer products. Republicans believe that, all facts to the contrary, the market is never wrong.

Democrats and Republicans are both capable of bringing us a balanced budget. Both can slash red tape. Both can help strengthen the family. But only we Democrats have the vision of a society where everyone—rich, poor, young, old, native, immigrant, black, white, Christian, Jew, and each and every other group that resides on this glorious piece of real estate we call the United States—has a chance to live a safe and comfortable life. We Democrats are the soul and conscience of this nation! We always have been—and, if we get our tent in order, we always will be.

Just as I started this book with a slap on the ass, here's yours! Get moving! No one's going to do it for us.

APPENDIX: MORE THINGS GOVERNMENT DOES RIGHT

❋ ❋ ❋ ❋ ❋ ❋ ❋

Ban on CFCs (first stage: 1990)

Description: The 1990 Clean Air Act Amendments began a phaseout of chlorofluorocarbons and several other chemicals that have ripped a hole in the earth's ozone layer, the part of the stratosphere that helps screen out dangerous ultraviolet radiation. The complete ban on CFC production begins this year.

Accomplishments: Thanks to the ban, the ozone layer should begin to recover around the turn of the century, helping to avoid further environmental and health damage. Industry has now developed alternatives to CFCs that are in many cases cheaper and better. This is one reason "why business doesn't back the GOP backlash on the ozone," as *Business Week* put it.[1] The ban is a model of how good science can lead to good public policy.

GOP: Many Republicans still say that CFCs are not the cause of our ozone problems. But right about the time when the Republicans were proposing to repeal the ban, the three scientists who discovered the link between CFCs and the ozone hole won the 1995 Nobel Prize in Chemistry for having "contributed to our salvation from a global environmental problem that could have catastrophic consequences."[2] So who are you gonna believe on this one, the Nobel Committee and a near-unanimous scientific community or House Republicans and Rush Limbaugh?

Brady Law (1993)

Description: The Brady Law requires a five-day waiting period and background checks when you go to buy a handgun. It was named for Jim Brady, who was permanently disabled when John Hinckley, Jr., opened fire on President Ronald Reagan.

Accomplishments: In the first nine months alone, 41,000 fugitives, drug users, stalkers, and convicted felons tried to buy a gun and were arrested or turned away.[3] God knows how many realized they shouldn't even bother. Of course, some of those people figured out how to get an illegal gun, but no matter how you add it up, we still stopped tens of thousands of felons from waltzing into Wal-Mart and getting themselves a piece.

GOP: Apparently, the Republicans think that government has no business keeping guns out of criminals' hands. They voted against the Brady Law to begin with, and they've been trying to repeal it ever since. For the life of me, I don't understand what the big deal is about waiting five days for a firearm. I just bought myself a pistol, and a pretty good one at that. It's a 38/357 Magnum. Around the same time, I bought a new washing machine and had to wait for delivery. If I could wait a week for a washing machine, I could sure as hell wait five days for a handgun!

Bureau of Economic Analysis (1953)

Description: The Bureau of Economic Analysis provides information on the state of the economy, from the rate of economic growth to the size of the trade deficit.

Accomplishments: Without the BEA, we wouldn't know too much about how the economy is doing. And that doesn't just mean that columnists like Robert Samuelson would have nothing to write about. Congress, the executive branch, the Federal Reserve, the stock and bond markets, private industry, pretty much our entire economy depends on the information the BEA provides. And private industry simply does not have the ability to do the BEA's job.

GOP: The Republicans want to cut the Bureau's budget at a time when it can least afford it. Now I could tell you what a stupid idea that is, but why not let a leading business publication say it instead. Here's *Business Week,* in an editorial called "Good Numbers Are Worth a Good Deal": "What use is an Information Age if the information is bad? That's what we may get if Washington cuts the budget of the Bureau of Economic Analysis. . . . Bad idea."[4]

Consumer Product Safety Commission (1972)

Description: The Consumer Product Safety Commission is responsible for making sure that more than 15,000 consumer products don't jeopardize our health or safety.

Accomplishments: Whether it is recalling skirts that catch fire or convincing children's clothing manufacturers to stop making drawstrings that strangle kids, the CPSC is always working to get dangerous products off the market. Every year, consumer products cause 21,700 deaths and 28.6 million injuries, costing us about $200 billion.[5] Imagine how much worse it would be without a watchdog to keep the industries honest. Nancy Steorts, a Reagan administration official, recently wrote a letter to *The Washington Times* with this heavy-duty endorsement: "Consumers benefit greatly from the work that the CPSC does. . . . The CPSC worries about safety for them and makes sure that corporations, which have not caught onto the new trends, are held accountable."[6]

GOP: Republicans want to cut funding for the commission and hamstring its ability to come up with new consumer-product standards. They think that market forces are fine for making sure products are safe. As in, if enough babies die in defective cribs, manufacturers will eventually do something about it.

Cooperative Extension Service (1914)

Description: If you're from a small rural town like mine, the Cooperative Extension Service needs little introduction. But for the rest of you, here's the scoop: The CES gives farmers the best information and latest research on agriculture. Although there are only 170 full-time federal CES employees, states and counties supply more than 16,000, and there are roughly 3 million CES volunteers.

Accomplishments: The CES has helped make America's farmers the most productive in the world. As a result, we spend a smaller percentage of our incomes on food than any other country. Wayne Rasmussen, in a 1989 book on the CES, declared the program a winner: "The Cooperative Extension System today is a unique achievement in American education. It is an agency for change and problem solving, a catalyst for individual and group action. . . . Extension people remain among the unsung heroes of the nation."[7]

GOP: Surprise, surprise—the Republicans cut nearly $11 million from the CES budget this year alone.

Direct Student Loans (1992)

Description: Used to be that in order to get a student loan, you had to go to a bank, even though it was the federal government that backed the loan. The government took the risk, but the banks got the profit. Sound fair to you? With direct loans, we cut out the middleman.

Accomplishments: Direct loans are popular with everyone but the banks. Here's *The New York Times* (front-page story): "The direct loans have proved popular with students because the money comes through faster, and with administrators, who have found them to be simpler to administer."[8] Jerome Supple, president of Southwest Texas State University: Direct loans is "a program that both saves money and improves service to its constituents."[9] John Van de Wetering, president of SUNY Brockport: "This is a system that works. It is more efficient for us, far better for the students than the previous process and saves taxpayers a significant amount of money."[10] The Congressional Budget Office said that if we stick with direct loans, we'll save $6.8 billion by the year 2000.[11]

GOP: The Republicans wanted to kill the program outright, but they ended up capping its growth, which will deny 2.5 million students direct-loan opportunities next year alone. There's only one explanation: They're going to bat for the banks, who just didn't want to lose that lucrative part of their business. In other words, they're taking money from kids and giving it to bankers. To try to hide that fact, the Republicans ordered the Congressional Budget Office to cook the books: They told them to factor in administrative costs for direct lending but not for the old system when evaluating the two programs. Republican Congressman Tom Petri (WI) was so disgusted he called it "blatant special interest protection."[12]

Family and Medical Leave Act (1993)

Description: If you decide to have a kid, or if your kid gets sick, or if your parents need a lot of your care and you have to take a little time off from work, you shouldn't have to worry about being fired. The Family and Medical Leave Act ensures that 42.5 million working Americans can get up to twelve weeks of unpaid leave for just these occasions.[13]

Accomplishments: It's worked just like we wanted it to, providing security and building stronger families. And what about all those horror stories the Republicans came up with when the President proposed this law? None of them happened. The Conference Board, a pro-business group, recently reported that 70 percent of employers said complying with the new law was easy or very easy.[14] And the Labor Policy Association found that 73 percent of employers thought the new law either had a positive effect on productivity or had no impact at all.[15]

GOP: Three-quarters of the Republicans in the last Congress voted against the act. And the Republicans in the current Congress are talking about cutting the enforcement budget.

Federal Home Loans (1934)

Description: The Federal Housing Administration guarantees mortgages for roughly half a million American home buyers each year. Two-thirds of those guaranteed loans go to first-time buyers.[16] With a federal guarantee, a mortgage is much easier to secure and cheaper to pay off.

Accomplishments: It used to be incredibly difficult for working families to take out a mortgage. But then the federal government decided to make home ownership a national priority. The FHA has now helped 23 million Americans to buy homes.[17] Thanks in part to the G.I. Bill's home loans and the FHA, home ownership has risen from 44 percent in the mid-1930s to 64 percent today, which puts us near the top in the world.[18]

GOP: Sen. Dole has proposed to cut the federal mortgage guarantee from 100 percent to 30 percent. His proposal would also deny FHA loans to any middle-class family making more than $38,000.

Food Labeling (1990)

Description: I love these new labels! It just couldn't be easier to figure out exactly what you're eating. Before these labels, everything was a big mishmash, and 40 percent of all processed foods sold in the United States had no nutritional labeling at all.[19]

Accomplishments: Well, I'll admit that I don't always want to know what's in my hot dog, but these labels are a great idea. Michael Jacobson of the Center for Science in the Public Interest described the new labels and the standards they're based on as "a public health milestone and a great victory for the American consumer."[20] I couldn't agree more. It used to be that you couldn't trust what you read on food packages. For example, "Ultra Fruit" oatmeal had no fruit in it. And the old system made it almost impossible to compare nutritional content unless you had a calculator and a degree in biochemistry. Now, competing products have the same realistic serving size, and all labels show percentages of daily requirements. And if a product says it has reduced fat or high fiber, you can be sure it means what it says.

GOP: The Republicans went along with this one, but now they want a regulatory moratorium that would stifle exactly this kind of regulatory innovation.

G.I. Bill (1944)

Description: At the end of World War II, Congress was worried about all those G.I.s coming back and not being able to find jobs. So they set up the G.I. Bill to pay for veterans to go to college and to help them get loans to buy homes and start businesses. The program is still going strong today.

Accomplishments: When Congress passed the G.I. Bill, it had no idea that it was making what may have been the single best investment in American history. George Bush gave this ringing endorsement: "The G.I. Bill changed the lives of millions by replacing old roadblocks with paths to opportunity. And, in so doing, it boosted America's workforce, it boosted America's economy, and really, it changed the life of our nation."[21] College enrollment shot up by 71 percent between 1939 and 1947. We've now had 20 million veterans go to college under the G.I. Bill. And more than 14 million Americans have bought homes using the bill's home loan guarantees.[22] The program has given us two Presidents, three Supreme Court Justices, and I can't count how many successful executives, civic leaders, and members of Congress—oh, and me, too (but don't hold that against it). Not a bad return on our investment. Kind of makes you think that investing in people ain't such a bad idea.

GOP: Senate Republicans tried to increase fees for those attending college on the G.I. Bill by $400 per person.

Green Lights Program (1991)

Description: A few years ago, the Environmental Protection Agency noticed that although new lighting technologies offered tremendous energy and cost savings, few people had heard about them, let alone bought them. The companies that produced these technologies were having trouble reaching businesses to show them the benefits, so they created the Green Lights Program to address this problem.

Accomplishments: Green Lights doesn't impose regulations. It offers help. It came up with software to allow buyers to assess potential energy savings, an informational campaign reaching the top executives at major corporations, even financing packages for nonprofit companies. Where they were installed, the new lighting technologies cut electricity demand by 47 percent. The program will end up saving $53 billion for companies.[23] The portion of that going back to the Treasury as federal taxes on higher profits will be more than enough to pay for the program's modest cost.

GOP: At one point last summer, Republicans proposed to scrap the whole program.

Human Genome Project (1990)

Description: Perhaps the greatest scientific endeavor in this country's history is the Human Genome Project. In the 1980s, researchers realized that they had the power to unlock the secrets of the human genetic code. All they lacked was money and organization. That's when the federal government stepped in. Medicine will never be the same.

Accomplishments: After five years, the project is under budget and ahead of schedule.[24] Researchers have already found genes that contribute to fifty diseases and have come up with tests for more than a dozen genetic disorders.[25]

GOP: The Republicans aren't cutting back on this project—too many people know how good it is. But the list of other valuable scientific research that the GOP is gutting is too long and horrifying to print here. I think you'll get the picture from the reaction of *The New York Times*'s editorial writers: "The magnitude of the House-passed cuts is shocking. Civilian research would fall over five years from about $32 billion to $25 billion, a 35 percent cut after accounting for inflation. Medical research, other than for AIDS, would fall by more than 25 percent."[26]

Interstate Highway System (1956)

Description: In 1956, under President Eisenhower, Congress passed the Federal-Aid Highway Act, and the modern interstate system was born. Today we have 42,795 miles of interstate highway without a single crossing or stoplight.[27]

Accomplishments: The next time you meet up with a devolution nut, propose the following: a race from Disneyworld to Disneyland. You take the federal interstate, and have your buddy take state roads (tell him to pack a couple of sandwiches). I can't say that I know a whole lot about infrastructure investments, but a magazine called *American City and County* sure does, and here's what it said about the interstate highways: "the greatest nonmilitary construction program ever undertaken in the world. . . . The interstate system has allowed a free flow of commerce unparalleled in world history."[28]

GOP: The Republicans are leaving the interstates alone.

Meals-On-Wheels (1972)

Description: Responding to reports of serious malnutrition among the elderly, Congress authorized a nutrition program that serves daily balanced meals in community centers and churches for senior citizens who can't fix their own. Meals-On-Wheels goes one step further, bringing lunch or dinner to the doors of those elderly people who cannot leave their homes.

Accomplishments: Nearly a million senior citizens depend on Meals-On-Wheels. Even Pat Buchanan's mom, who has now passed away, was a big fan of the program. She served as the chair of a Washington chapter. Meals-On-Wheels isn't just a federal program: State and local governments, corporations, community organizations, and the elderly it serves all contribute. In fact, recipients contributed $171 million in 1993 alone.[29]

GOP: Pat Buchanan's party thinks Meals-On-Wheels ought to be cut by 10 percent.

Mine Safety and Health Administration (1969)

Description: The Mine Safety and Health Administration is responsible for making sure that miners are protected from hazards such as fires, cave-ins, explosions, and black-lung disease.

Accomplishments: Since the 1960s, the fatality rate for coal miners has fallen by 400 percent.[30] MSHA deserves a heavy helping of the credit.

GOP: Republicans have proposed eliminating MSHA and having the Occupational Safety and Health Administration assume some of its responsibilities. Peter Kilborn of *The New York Times,* under the headline "Saving Money or Saving Lives: A Bill to Reduce Regulations Alarms Safety Experts," reported that the Republican bill would "shrink the agency, strip it of its independence, and inhibit its freedom to make unannounced inspections."[31] The bill would cut inspections of underground mines by 75 percent. It would eliminate fines for many violations and greatly reduce fines for others. A spokesman for the United Mine Workers put it this way: "Every meaningful penalty and means of enforcement would be stripped away."[32] Maybe that's why even the largest group representing the mine owners, the National Mining Association, has not come out in favor of the bill. How the Republicans can still go around claiming that they care about working people is beyond me.

Motor Voter (1993)

Description: The National Voter Registration Act allows you to register to vote when you go for a driver's license, through the mail, and at some public assistance offices.

Accomplishments: Has it worked? Here's what *The New York Times* said in a front-page story: "In what political experts say is the greatest expansion of voter rolls in the nation's history, more than 5 million Americans have registered to vote in the eight months since the National Voter Registration Act was enacted."[33] According to the League of Women Voters, the law will have added up to 20 million new registered voters by the 1996 election.[34]

GOP: Republicans hate this law, and it's no secret why. They think that it will add more Democrats than Republicans to the voting rolls.

National Biological Service (1993)

Description: The National Biological Service was created to bring biological research at the Department of the Interior under one roof. Its research is aimed at finding environmentally sound ways of promoting economic development.

Accomplishments: The NBS has provided valuable information to America's ranchers on grasses and weeds that interfere with cattle grazing. It is doing research on Great Lakes fish stocks to avoid overfishing, which left the New England coast with a decimated fish population and sent many commercial fishermen into financial ruin. It has assisted International Paper in improving the company's environmental policies, averting environmental problems that would be costly to both the company and the rest of us.

GOP: Republicans have moved to cut the service's budget by 20 percent.

National Crime Information Center (1967)

Description: The National Crime Information Center is a federal computer clearinghouse that provides instant information on crimes and criminals to cops and criminal justice agencies all over the United States and Canada. The NCIC database tracks almost 400,000 people wanted by the police, and it receives 1.3 million inquiries every day.[35]

Accomplishments: Not many people had heard of the center until it helped nab a guy named Timothy McVeigh. You see, less than two hours after the Oklahoma City bombing, McVeigh had been pulled over by a state trooper near Perry, Oklahoma, for driving without license plates and been arrested when the officer found a semiautomatic pistol in the car. The cops loaded McVeigh's name and description into the NCIC database, and that's how the FBI knew just where to find him when he became a suspect in the bombing. If it hadn't been for that database, McVeigh might be sipping margaritas in Mexico right now.

GOP: It looks like the Republicans have the good sense to leave this one alone.

National Health Service Corps (1970)

Description: From rural Utah to the South Bronx, many small towns and inner cities simply cannot attract doctors to serve their communities. The National Health Service Corps offers doctors and nurses the chance to have their medical school loans paid off and receive a small salary in return for a two-year commitment to provide medical care in an underserved area.

Accomplishments: Nearly 4 million Americans who would not otherwise have access to health care are served by NHSC doctors and nurses.[36] And that's just from those currently enrolled in the corps. More than half of those who serve stay on in the community after their required service is over.

GOP: Republicans tried to cut the NHSC in half. Did they really think the TV show *Northern Exposure* or the free market is going to get enough doctors to work in frigid Alaska or the desperately poor areas of West Virginia?

National Parks (1916)

Description: The national park system is made up of 369 parks, covering 83 million acres. The parks both preserve and make accessible some of the nation's most beautiful land.

Accomplishments: In 1994, there were over 268 million visitors to our national parks. And there's no bloated bureaucracy here; the National Park Service uses more than four times as many volunteers as employees.

GOP: The Republicans want to open more park land to logging and mining. They want to cut the Park Service's budget by $100 million this year. One Republican, Rep. Joel Hefley (CO), even wants to form a national park *closing* commission.[37]

National Weather Service (1890)

Description: Besides letting you know whether you need an umbrella, the National Weather Service provides vital information for farmers, sailors, and pilots.

Accomplishments: A new computer radar system being introduced now, which can forecast hurricane paths earlier and ten miles closer to their true path, will reduce costs by $10 million every time there's a hurricane evacuation.[38] The NWS is also closing 200 weather stations, because computers can now do the job better and cheaper. That's going to save the taxpayers $180 million.[39]

GOP: The House Republicans don't think it's the government's business whether farmers lose crops or airplanes fly into thunderstorms. They want to privatize much of the NWS.

Peace Corps (1961)

Description: John F. Kennedy established the Peace Corps, a program that sends 7,000 Americans every year to developing countries and the former Eastern Bloc to help with everything from irrigation to health care.

Accomplishments: More than 140,000 Americans have served in the Peace Corps in 120 countries. Volunteers do strenuous work in difficult conditions and make only $225 a month. Yet somehow there's a six- to nine-month waiting list. And here's a piece of interesting trivia: It was Peace Corps volunteers in Nigeria who first taught Houston Rockets center Hakeem Olajuwon how to play basketball.

GOP: Even Jesse Helms, who is ready to skip out on most of our foreign-aid commitments, has called the Peace Corps "one of the best investments this government makes."[40] I guess that's why the Republicans only want to cut its budget by some 10 percent.

Reemployment Screening (1993)

Description: A pilot state and federal initiative to "profile" electronically newly unemployed workers to identify those likely to be long-term unemployed and give them special job search assistance.

Accomplishments: Workers singled out for assistance found new jobs, on average, up to four weeks sooner than similar individuals who were not. Each dollar spent on search assistance saved the government two dollars, by shortening the length of unemployment.[41]

GOP: The Republicans have underfunded the unemployment insurance program and employment services. That means less money for one-stop reemployment centers, more delinquent unemployment-tax payments, and less money for reemployment training and profiling.

School Lunches and Breakfasts (1946)

Description: The school lunch and breakfast programs provide proper nutrition for schoolchildren who might not otherwise get it. Kids in or near poverty are eligible for free breakfasts and lunches; those slightly better off are eligible for reduced-cost meals.

Accomplishments: Children who participate in school lunch programs are better nourished than those who don't. Low-income kids depend on the programs for a third to half of their daily nutrition.[42] And Mom was right: Breakfast is important. Poor elementary school kids in the programs did better in school and had better attendance records than those who did not participate.[43]

GOP: Not so long ago, a program as sensible as this was assured bipartisan support in Congress. Now the right-wingers just don't care what works and what doesn't. The House Republicans want to eliminate nutritional requirements, scrap the requirement that children in poverty receive free school lunches, and allow 20 percent of the funds to be spent by states on other, unrelated block-grant programs. If the Republican plan is enacted millions of children will lose their subsidies and be served less-nutritious meals. If last time around they were calling ketchup a vegetable, I bet this time around tropical-flavored LifeSavers will be considered a fruit.

School-to-Work (1994)

Description: The jobs that used to lead a new high school graduate onto a path toward middle-class comfort are few and far between. Workers without much in the way of skills are increasingly locked into low-wage jobs with few benefits, minimal job security, and little hope of real advancement. The School-to-Work program attempts to bridge the gap between school and the work world for those who don't go on to college. It keeps students interested in school and gives them the skills, experience, and links to the job market that open the door to a good job and a good future.

Accomplishments: This isn't some new Washington bureaucracy. The program provides seed money for projects run at the state and local levels. Participation is voluntary, although states and localities are lining up to get on board. And the program will phase out of existence in 2001, its work completed. School-to-Work has only been around for a year, but we're already seeing success stories roll in. One study in Oregon found that the program cut the dropout rate by 62 percent.[44] Our major economic competitors around the world have been smart enough to do this kind of thing for years.

GOP: It doesn't matter that it's a damn good idea, supported by many top corporate executives. It was President Clinton's damn good idea, so Newt Gingrich wants to cut its budget by a quarter.

Senior Community Service Employment Program (1965)

Description: Through this winner program, a hundred thousand poor senior citizens receive the minimum wage to do needed jobs in their communities. The Senior Community Service Employment Program is administered by ten nonprofit groups that match people with jobs.

Accomplishments: For a cost of only $4,420 per year, we can keep a senior citizen out of poverty, off welfare, and in a productive job.

Let me give the floor to Peter Kilborn of *The New York Times:* "[It] provides work, wages and hope. . . . The program has regularly met the performance goals that Congress sets for it. . . . It is also cheap."[45]

GOP: At one point last year, the Republicans wanted to cut this one altogether. They later backed down from that intention, but they're still trying to make substantial cuts. Ten thousand elderly workers will be denied their jobs.[46]

Sesame Street *(1969)*

Description: Sesame Street is seen by 120 million viewers in 130 countries, one of those viewers being my little daughter. It is just one of the Public Broadcasting Service's many educational and informative programs that provide an alternative to the daytime trash on the commercial channels.

Accomplishments: Sesame Street and other quality kids' shows on PBS raise scores on tests of math, reading, and overall school readiness—even years later.[47] The kids who watch these shows spend more time reading and doing other educational activities.[48] *Sesame Street* alone has been honored with sixty-two Emmys and dozens of educational awards. And don't let them tell you that PBS is a subsidy for yuppies: Most viewers come from households that make less than $40,000.[49]

GOP: If you thought Oscar was a grouch, think about Newt. While he was out there decrying all the violence our kids see on the commercial channels, he wanted to eliminate funding for PBS. Luckily, we got him to back down. Now he just wants to cut PBS funding by about 20 percent.

Smokey Bear *(1944)*

Description: Smokey is part of the Forest Service's fire prevention and control efforts. His job is to raise awareness of the causes of forest fires through public-service commercials and billboards.

Accomplishments: When some people think of Smokey, they think of a friendly bear who hangs around in national parks. When

I think of him, I remember my drill instructor with that hat sticking out into my face. But the best way to think of Smokey is as a damn effective guy. Fifty years ago, forest fires destroyed about 30 million acres of land every year. With the help of Smokey, the Forest Service has cut the losses down to about 4 million acres. Why give so much credit to a guy in a bear suit? Well, the Forest Service has concluded that soon after Smokey hit the airwaves the rate of accidental fires per 1,000 visitors began to decline in a big way.

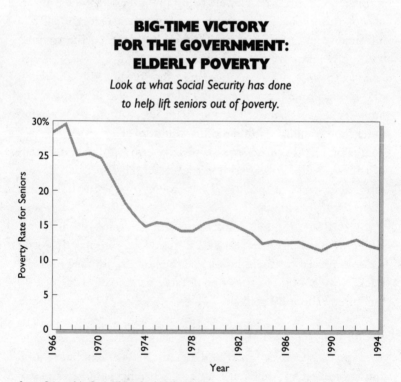

BIG-TIME VICTORY FOR THE GOVERNMENT: ELDERLY POVERTY

Look at what Social Security has done to help lift seniors out of poverty.

Source: Bureau of the Census, *Current Population Survey.*

GOP: The way Republicans look at problems, I wouldn't be surprised if they wanted to get rid of Smokey: We've still got fires, so the bear must not be working.

Social Security (1935)

Description: Social Security ensures that older Americans have a guaranteed source of income after a lifetime of work.

Accomplishments: The reduction in elderly poverty is the single largest accomplishment of Lyndon Johnson's Great Society. In 1966, almost 30 percent of our senior citizens lived in poverty. Thanks to LBJ's expansion of Social Security, that is down to 12 percent today. The Social Security Administration also happens to run a very tight ship. Last May, *Business Week* published a comprehensive ranking of telephone customer-service operations. Social Security was ranked number one, with the most "courteous, knowledgeable, and efficient" service in the nation. It beat out such venerable private companies as L. L. Bean, FedEx, and Disney.[50]

GOP: Right-wingers have learned not to say too much about Social Security, but they hate it. I'm not talking about some fringe element within the party. One of Bob Dole's top advisers on the issue recently came out in favor of privatizing Social Security. And Dole appointed that same adviser to the bipartisan council that is supposed to produce a plan for Social Security's future. When reporters confronted the Majority Leader's staff and asked them to state their boss's position on privatization, they refused to comment.[51] And what's so bad about privatization? It might work okay for those people who have lots to contribute, but what would happen to the millions of Americans whose wages are stagnating or declining? If you're living hand-to-mouth and can't contribute much, you aren't going to be collecting much on retirement. Privatization would mean that elderly poverty would soar once again.

WIC (1972)

Description: WIC, the Special Supplemental Food Program for Women and Infant Children, makes sure that pregnant women and newborns get enough to eat.

Accomplishments: Before someone starts calling me a socialist for thinking that pregnant women and children shouldn't starve, I should say that a study in 1990 found that the government saves two to four dollars on Medicaid for every dollar spent on WIC.[52] The General Accounting Office, the watchdog of Congress, found that the return was three dollars for every dollar spent.[53] Healthy kids and money saved.

GOP: First, House Republicans tried to limit the number of people who could be helped by WIC, but Democrats blocked that effort. Then the Republicans voted to replace the WIC entitlement with a portion of a block grant. And don't forget about the Republicans' slimy and costly decision to get rid of competitive bidding in the WIC program—just one more way they could help out the special interests at the expense of the rest of us.

NOTES

✿ ✿ ✿ ✿

Introduction

1. Joseph M. Giordano, "Facts for the President's Fable," *Los Angeles Times,* Sept. 18, 1984.

Carville's Rapid-Response Team Comes to Your Backyard Barbecue

1. Press packet handed out by Dr. Laura D'Andrea Tyson and Dr. Alice Rivlin, Nov. 18, 1995.

2. Real GDP growth between 1980 and 1990 was 2.6 percent per year. Real GDP growth between 1970 and 1980 was 2.8 percent per year. Based on data from the Department of Commerce, Bureau of Economic Analysis.

3. Paul Krugman, *Peddling Prosperity* (New York: W. W. Norton, 1994), pp. 17, 126.

4. Alan S. Blinder, *Hard Heads, Soft Hearts: Tough-minded Economics for a Just Society* (Reading, Mass.: Addison-Wesley, 1987), p. 89.

5. William Greider, "The Education of David Stockman," *Atlantic Monthly,* Dec. 1981.

6. John Rutledge and Deborah Allen, "We Should Love the Trade Deficit," *Fortune,* Feb. 29, 1988.

7. Based on data from the Bureau of Labor Statistics, Current Employment Statistics survey.

8. Ibid.

9. Martin Anderson, "The Great American Tax Debate," *Policy Review,* Spring 1991.

10. William Safire, in debate with James Carville, Pacific Univ., Forest Grove, Ore., Feb. 21, 1995.

11. Benjamin Friedman, *Day of Reckoning* (New York: Vintage Books, 1988), p. 128.

12. Ibid.

13. Safire in debate with Carville.

14. House Appropriations Committee, *Regular, Annual, Supplemental, and Deficiency Appropriations Bills: Comparison of Administration Budget Requests and Appropriations Enacted,* Sept. 30, 1994.

15. Ibid.

16. David A. Stockman, "America Is Not Overspending; North America: The Big Engine That Couldn't," *New Perspectives Quarterly,* Mar. 22, 1993.

17. Ronald Reagan, "Hurry Up and Wait," *Wall Street Journal,* July 8, 1993.

18. Congressional Budget Office, *The 1993 Green Book* (Washington, D.C.: Government Printing Office), tables 11 and 26.

19. Ibid.

20. Robert L. Bartley, *The Seven Fat Years—and How to Do It Again* (New York: Free Press, 1992), p. x.

21. Ibid., p. 15.

22. Rush Limbaugh, *The Way Things Ought to Be* (New York: Pocket Books, 1992), p. 288.

23. Ronald G. Shafer, "Minor Memos," *Wall Street Journal,* June 23, 1995.

24. Robert Reich, testimony before the Joint Economic Committee, Feb. 23, 1995.

25. Robert Moffit and Barbara Wolfe, "The Effect of the Medicaid Program on Welfare Participation and Labor Supply," *Review of Economics and Statistics,* Nov. 1992, pp. 615–26.

26. Nancy Gibbs, "Worker Harder, Getting Nowhere," *Time,* July 3, 1995.

27. Mickey Kaus, "Bastards: The Right Abandons Welfare," *New Republic,* Feb. 21, 1994.

28. Sharon Parrott (Center on Budget and Policy Priorities), personal communication to author, Aug. 1995.

29. Based on data from the Bureau of the Census, Current Population Survey.

30. Peter T. Kilborn, "Take This Job; Up from Welfare: It's Harder and Harder," *New York Times,* Apr. 16, 1995.

31. Robert Rector, testimony before the House Subcommittee on Human Resources, Aug. 9, 1994.

32. Lawrence Mishel and Jared Bernstein, *The State of Working America: 1994–95* (Washington, D.C.: Economic Policy Institute, 1994), p. 316.

33. Phil Gramm, speech at Liberty Univ., Lynchburg, Va., May 5, 1995.

34. Sharon Parrott, personal communication to author, Aug. 1995.

35. Gramm, speech at Liberty Univ.

36. Karen Hosler, "Dole Begins Uphill Battle for His Welfare Reforms," *Baltimore Sun,* Aug. 8, 1995.

37. Judith Havemann and Barbara Vobejda, "Moderates Kill 'Family Cap' in Senate Welfare Measure," *Washington Post,* Sept. 14, 1995.

38. Barbara Vobejda, "N.J. Welfare 'Cap' Has No Effect on Births, Study Finds," *Washington Post,* June 21, 1995.

39. William J. Bennett, "End Welfare for Single Women Having Children," *USA Today,* Feb. 1, 1994.

40. Tufts Univ. Center on Hunger, Poverty, and Nutrition Policy, *Statement on Key Welfare Reform Issues: The Empirical Evidence,* 1995, pp. 4, 5.

41. G. Acs, *The Impact of AFDC on Young Women's Childbearing Decisions* (Washington, D.C.: Urban Institute, May 1994).

42. P. K. Robins and P. Fronstin, *Welfare Benefits and Family-Size Decisions of Never-Married Women,* Institute for Research on Poverty Discussion Paper 1022-93 (Univ. of Wisconsin, Madison, Sept. 1993).

43. J. Mauldon and S. Miller, *Child-Bearing Desires and Sterilization Among United States Women: Patterns by Income and AFDC Recipiency,* Working Paper 209 (Univ. of California, Berkeley, Graduate School of Public Policy, Aug. 1994).

44. Charles Murray, "Welfare and the Family: The U.S. experience," *Journal of Labor Economics,* vol. II, no. 1, 1993, pp. S224–S262.

45. Susan Molinari, "Local Woes Need Local Cures," *Daily News* (New York), July 9, 1995.

46. Newt Gingrich, "All of Us Together . . . Must Totally Remake the Federal Government," *Washington Post,* Apr. 8, 1995.

47. Barbara Vobejda, "Gauging Welfare's Role in Motherhood," *Washington Post,* June 2, 1994.

48. Based on data from the Bureau of the Census, Current Population Survey.

49. Ibid.

50. "House Passes GOP Welfare Reform Bill; 'Contract with America' Pledge Sails Through on a 234–199 Near-Party-Line Vote," *Chicago Tribune,* Mar. 24, 1995.

51. Lee Rainwater and Timothy Smeeding, *Doing Poorly: The Real Income of American Children in a Comparative Perspective,* Luxembourg Income Study Working Paper 127, Aug. 1995.

52. *Wall Street Journal*/NBC News poll, as cited in "Wanted: Welfare That Works" (editorial), *Roanoke Times & World News,* May 22, 1995.

53. Jeffrey Lehman and Sheldon Danziger, "Ending Welfare as We Know It: Values, Economics, and Politics," University of Michigan Working Paper, Dec. 1994, p. 10.

54. *The Late Edition* (5:00 P.M. ET), CNN, Jan. 1, 1995.

55. David Whitman, "Let Fifty Flowers Bloom," *U.S. News & World Report,* Mar. 27, 1995.

56. Michael Rezendes, "Doing the Minimum: Clinton Wants a Higher Minimum Wage," *Boston Globe,* Jan. 29, 1995.

57. David Card and Alan B. Krueger, "Minimum Wage and Employment: A Case Study of the Fast-Food Industry in New Jersey and Pennsylvania," *American Economic Review,* vol. 84, 1994, pp. 772–93.

58. James Risen, "Obscure GOP Plan May Be Tax Windfall for Business," *Los Angeles Times,* Apr. 5, 1995.

59. Lucinda Harper, "GOP Pushing Big Corporate Tax Break in the Form of Depreciation Changes," *Wall Street Journal,* Dec. 5, 1994.

60. Iris Lav, Cindy Mann, and Pauline Abernathy, *Tax Proposals in the Contract with America: Assessing the Long-term Impact* (Washington, D.C.: Center on Budget and Policy Priorities, Jan. 13, 1995).

61. Office of Tax Analysis, Department of the Treasury, *A Preliminary Analysis of a Flat-Rate Consumption Tax,* 1995.

62. Robert E. Hall and Alvin Rabushka, *Low Tax, Simple Tax, Flat Tax* (New York: McGraw-Hill, 1983), p. 58.

63. Based on calculations from Citizens for Tax Justice, Washington, D.C.

64. Richard Armey, testimony before the Senate Finance Committee, Apr. 5, 1995.

65. Based on calculations from Citizens for Tax Justice, Washington, DC. Analysis assumes revenue neutrality.

66. James Risen, "Bill Who?" *Financial World,* Dec. 6, 1994.

67. David S. Broder, "Less and Less for the Poor," *Washington Post,* Oct. 1, 1995.

68. Peter A. Brown, "The Tax Debate: 'Fairer, Flatter'; U.S. May Deduct IRS from Life," Scripps Howard News Service, Apr. 16, 1995.

69. Robert McIntyre and Jeff Spinner, *130 Reasons Why We Need Tax Reform* (Washington, D.C.: Citizens for Tax Justice, 1986).

70. "Taxed and Spent: Failures of Bill Clinton's Budget Plan," *National Review*, Aug. 23, 1993.

71. Based on data from the Bureau of Economic Analysis, National Income and Product Accounts.

72. Ibid.

73. Based on data from Dun and Bradstreet.

74. Based on data from the Bureau of Labor Statistics, Current Employment Statistics survey.

75. Based on data from the Department of the Treasury.

76. Mona Charen, "Flat-out Fantasy from Gephardt," *Washington Times*, July 12, 1995.

77. *News* (8:06 P.M. ET), CNN, June 27, 1995.

78. *Meet the Press*, NBC News, Dec. 4, 1994.

79. Michael Kramer, "Newt's Believe It or Not," *Time*, Dec. 19, 1994.

80. *The Late Edition* (5:00 P.M. ET), CNN, Jan. 1, 1995.

81. Richard K. Armey, *The Freedom Revolution: The New Republican House Majority Leader Tells Why Big Government Failed . . .* (Washington, D.C.: Regnery, 1995), p. 316.

82. Newt Gingrich (with David Drake and Marianne Gingrich), *Window of Opportunity: A Blueprint for the Future* (New York: T. Doherty Associates and Baen Enterprises, 1984), p. 97.

83. Gramm, speech at Liberty Univ.

84. President William J. Clinton, speech to the Democratic Leadership Council, Washington, D.C., Nov. 13, 1995.

85. Based on data from the Bureau of Labor Statistics, Current Employment Statistics survey.

86. Based on data from the Bureau of Economic Analysis, National Income and Product Accounts.

87. *Crossfire*, CNN, Jan. 11, 1995.

Things Government Does Right

1. Rush Limbaugh, *See, I Told You So* (New York: Pocket Books, 1993), p. 7.

2. Lawrence A. Kudlow, "Fed Up: Replacing the Current U.S. Monetary System with One That Limits Inflation," *National Review*, Oct. 10, 1994.

3. Michael Wines, "Why Liberalism Isn't Allowed to Die," *New York Times*, Sept. 10, 1995.

4. Quoted by Bruce Moyer in testimony before the House Committee on Government Reform, Oct. 13, 1995.

5. Stephen Barr, "Study Cites 'Impressive Results' but Calls for Strategy to Win Congressional Support," *Washington Post,* Aug. 19, 1994.

6. National Performance Review, *Common Sense Government: Works Better and Costs Less,* Sept. 1995.

7. The White House, *Briefing Papers on Select Administration Policies,* prepared for the 1995 Southern Economic Conference of the President, March 1995.

8. John Breaux press conference on the Republican budget, May 18, 1995.

9. Michael Clements, "Treasury: GOP Plan Hits Families," *USA Today,* Sept. 18, 1995.

10. Steven Barnett, "Benefits of Compensatory Preschool Education," *Journal of Human Resources,* Spring 1992.

11. The White House, "Impact of the Republican Budget," Nov. 30, 1995.

12. *AmeriCorps: First Year Review* (Washington, D.C.: Corporation for National Service, 1995).

13. Ibid.

14. Ibid.

15. E. J. Dionne, Jr., "AmeriCorps: Let It Live," *Washington Post,* Aug. 8, 1995.

16. Daniel Franklin, "The FEMA Phoenix," *Washington Monthly,* July 1995.

17. Ibid.

18. Gregg Easterbrook, *A Moment on the Earth* (New York: Viking, 1995), p. 628.

19. John Skow, "Earth Day Blues," *Time,* Apr. 24, 1995.

20. Carol Browner, White House press briefing, Aug. 8, 1995.

21. Gareth Cook, "Laws for Sale: Republicans in Congress Let Lobbyists Write Laws," *Washington Monthly,* July 1995.

22. Laurie Garrett, "The World's Lone Civilian Lab That Can Handle the Deadliest Microbes May Be Strained to the Danger Point by the Ebola Outbreak," *Newsday,* June 6, 1995.

23. Shannon Brownlee, "Tales from the Hot Zone," *U.S. News & World Report,* Mar. 27, 1995.

24. David S. Broder, "Scare Politics of Medicare," *Washington Post,* July 26, 1995.

25. Congressional Budget Office, projected baselines for fiscal years 1996 to 2002.

26. The White House, "Impact of the Republican Budget," Nov. 30, 1995.

27. Newt Gingrich, remarks to the National Governors' Association, Jan. 31, 1995.

28. Bob Hahn, personal communication to author, Feb. 1995.

29. Michael Belliveau (executive director, Citizens for Environment), personal communication to author, Feb. 1995.

30. Barbara Berney, "Round and Round It Goes: The Epidemiology of Childhood Lead Poisoning, 1950–1990," *Milbank Quarterly,* Mar. 22, 1993.

31. Ibid.

32. Samuel S. Epstein, *The Politics of Cancer* (New York: Anchor Press, Doubleday, 1979); Barry Commoner, *Making Peace with the Planet* (New York: Pantheon Books, 1990).

It's **Still** *the Economy, Stupid*

1. Based on data for full-time workers from the Bureau of Labor Statistics, *Current Population Survey.*

2. Peter Gottschalk and Timothy Smeeding, *Cross-national Comparisons of Levels and Trends in Inequality,* Luxembourg Income Study Working Paper 126, July 1995.

3. Edward N. Wolff, "How the Pie Is Sliced: America's Growing Concentration of Wealth," *American Prospect,* Summer 1995.

4. Bureau of the Census, *Current Population Survey.*

5. Frank Levy, unpublished tabulations, 1995.

6. Paul Krugman, "The Wealth Gap Is Real and It's Growing," *New York Times,* Aug. 21, 1995.

7. Robert J. Samuelson, "The Nadir of His Presidency," *Washington Post,* Dec. 21, 1994.

8. Bureau of Labor Statistics, *Report on the American Workforce,* 1994, p. 69.

9. George F. Will, "The Great Redistributor," *Washington Post,* Apr. 23, 1995.

10. David Wessel, "Greenspan Predicts Revival of Growth without Any Acceleration of Inflation," *Wall Street Journal,* July 20, 1995.

11. John Cassidy, "Who Killed the Great Middle Class?" *New Yorker,* Oct. 16, 1995.

12. James Fallows, personal communication to author, May 1995.

13. Based on data from the Bureau of Labor Statistics, *Current Population Survey.*

14. Robert Reich, speech at Center for National Policy, Washington, D.C., "Frayed-Collar Workers in Gold-Plated Times: The State of the American Workforce 1995," Aug. 31, 1995.

15. International Monetary Fund, World Economic Outlook, Fall 1995.

Daddies Matter: A Long Overdue Chat on the Family

1. Pat Robertson, Christian Coalition fund-raising letter, May 1995.

2. Frank Rich, "Gingrich Family Values," *New York Times,* May 14, 1995.

3. Newt Gingrich, quoted in Dale Russakoff, "Gingrich Lobs a Few More Bombs," *Washington Post,* Nov. 10, 1994.

4. Patrick Buchanan, quoted in Rupert Cornwell, "Bush Camp Perfects Battle Plan," *Independent,* Aug. 19, 1992.

5. Rich Bond, quoted in Gwen Ifill, "The Democrats; Clinton Shrugs Off Republican Attacks On His Wife's Work," *New York Times,* Aug. 13, 1992.

6. Newt Gingrich, *To Renew America* (New York: HarperCollins, 1995), p. 78.

7. *Dateline NBC,* Nov. 15, 1994.

8. Robert Reich, remarks before the National Baptist Convention, San Diego, Cal., June 21, 1995.

They Call Me Mr. Carville

1. Rochelle Sharpe, "Primary Lessons: Federal Education Law Becomes Hot Target of Wary Conservatives," *Wall Street Journal,* Aug. 30, 1995, p. A1.

2. Ibid.

3. Rene Sanchez, "Education Goals Program Targeted For Early Demise," *Washington Post,* Sept. 26, 1995.

4. Rob Chaney, "Woman Claims She Was Sex Slave for Goals 2000 Program," *Bozeman Daily Chronicle,* Sept. 13, 1995.

5. Star Parker, "Escaping the Welfare Stranglehold," speech delivered at the Christian Coalition Conference, Washington, D.C., Sept. 8–9, 1995.

6. Pat Robertson, *The Turning Tide* (Dallas: Word, 1993), p. 239.

7. Kevin B. Smith and Kenneth J. Meier, *The Case Against School Choice* (Armonk, N.Y.: M. E. Sharpe, 1995), p. 19.

8. V. Dion Haynes, "Foes Attack School-Voucher Plan; Programs Successes, Legality Questioned," *Chicago Tribune,* Feb. 9, 1995.

9. Mana Koklanaris, "Fairfax School Tops Ment Scholars List," *Washington Times,* Sept. 13, 1995.

10. Albert Shanker, *Myths and Facts about Private School Choice* (Washington, D.C.: American Federation of Teachers, Fall 1993), p. 15.

11. James Bock, " 'Sweetheart Deal of a Lifetime' Has a Pricetag; City Gave Extra $18 Million to Manage EAI Schools, Leaving Others with Less," *Baltimore Sun,* June 5, 1995.

12. Gary Gately, "EAI Schools' Test Scores Fall Short," *Baltimore Sun,* Oct. 18, 1995.

13. "New Report Questions Cost of School Management Firm," *Star Tribune,* June 7, 1995.

14. Gary Gately and JoAnna Daemmrich, "EAI Schools Fail to Match Citywide Attendance Gains," *Baltimore Sun*, Oct. 29, 1995.

15. M. William Salganik, "Privatization Suffers Blow with EAI Loss," *Baltimore Sun,* Dec. 2, 1995.

16. Elizabeth Gleick, "Privatized Lives," *Time,* Nov. 13, 1995.

17. Ibid.

18. John Larrabee, "The Business of School Reform," *USA Today,* June 7, 1995.

19. Ibid.

20. Rick Green, "EAI: Trying to Make the Grade," *Hartford Courant,* June 25, 1995.

21. Maria Newman, "Cortines Hails Efforts to Push Tough Classes," *New York Times,* May 9, 1995.

22. Ibid.

23. Vivian S. Toy, "Test Scores in New York City Rise for First Time in Six Years," *New York Times,* June 13, 1995.

24. *The Land Grant Tradition* (Washington, D.C.: National Association of State Universities and Land-Grant Colleges, Mar. 1995), p. 5.

Why the Best Plan Didn't Win

1. Edwin Chen, "Health Plan Is 'Superior' to Alternatives, First Lady Says; She is Cheered by GOP Senators," *Los Angeles Times,* Oct. 30, 1993.

2. William Kristol, "Defeating President Clinton's Health Care Proposal," memorandum for the Project for the Republican Future, Dec. 2, 1993.

3. Stefani G. Kopence, "Gramm Criticizes Health Plan," *Austin-American Statesman,* Feb. 7, 1994.

4. Phyllis Schlafly, Eagle Forum fund-raising letter, Feb. 1994.

5. Peter Jennings, speech accepting Paul White Award at the Radio Television News Directors Association, Sept. 9, 1995.

6. William Raspberry, "Blow-by-Blow Coverage," *Washington Post,* Oct. 30, 1995.

7. Tom Hamburger, "Coverage on Health Care Confuses More Than It Clarifies," *Minneapolis Star-Tribune,* Oct. 24, 1994.

8. James Fallows, "A Triumph of Misinformation," *Atlantic Monthly,* Jan. 1995.

9. Hilary Stout, "Many Don't Realize It's the Clinton Plan They Like," *Wall Street Journal,* Mar. 10, 1995.

10. Based on data from the Bureau of the Census, Current Population Survey.

11. Udayou Gupta and Jeanne Saddler, "Small Business Sees Burden Getting Lighter," *Wall Street Journal,* Sept. 13, 1993.

12. "Health Overhaul Opponents Tied to Gifts," *New York Times,* Aug. 13, 1995.

13. Katharine Q. Seelye, "Lobbyists Are the Loudest in the Health Care Debate," *New York Times,* Aug. 16, 1994.

14. *Congressional Record,* Apr. 8, 1965, pp. 7389–90.

15. *Congressional Record,* Sept. 2, 1964, pp. 21, 314–21, 315.

16. *Congressional Record,* Apr. 8, 1965, p. 7434.

17. Pete Stark, "The Politics of Medicare," *JAMA,* July 19, 1995, p. 274.

18. "GOP Medicare Plan Passed by the House," *Wall Street Journal,* Oct. 20, 1995.

19. "Class Conflict in Washington" (editorial), *New York Times,* Oct. 22, 1995.

20. Bob Dole, speech to American Conservative Union forum, Washington, D.C., Oct. 24, 1995.

21. Newt Gingrich, speech to Blue Cross/Blue Shield Conference, Washington, D.C., Oct. 25, 1995.

22. Judith Havemann and Spencer Rich, "Wording of House GOP's Medicare Memo Upsets Senior Citizen Groups," *Washington Post,* July 23, 1995.

23. Keith Bradsher, "Rise in Uninsured Becomes an Issue in Medicaid Fight," *New York Times,* Aug. 27, 1995.

A (Too) Brief Note on Why I Am Discouraged About Race
1. Remarks by President Clinton, University of Texas, Oct. 16, 1995.
2. Ibid.

Conclusion: It's Up To Us
1. *Inside Politics,* CNN, Nov. 4, 1994.
2. William Kristol, "The Erosion of Liberalism," *USA Today* magazine, Mar. 1995.
3. Greg McDonald, "In Praising FDR Years, Clinton Asks Congress to Protect Legacy," *Houston Chronicle,* Apr. 13, 1995.
4. Arthur M. Schlesinger, Jr., "The 'Hundred Days' of FDR," *New York Times,* Apr. 10, 1983.
5. Arthur M. Schlesinger, Jr., "The Big-Government Debate in the United States," *Daily Yomiuri,* May 8, 1995.
6. Robert G. Torricelli, "Forty Years and Proud of 'Em: An Unrepentant Democrat Looks Back," *Washington Post,* Jan. 5, 1995.
7. "A Job Half-well Done" (editorial), *Los Angeles Times,* July 30, 1995.
8. Brad Knickerbocker, "As Drivers Shift to Guzzlers, Nation's Fuel Efficiency Stalls," *Christian Science Monitor,* Oct. 6, 1995.
9. Environmental Protection Agency, Office of Public Affairs, "Clean Air Act: Success Stories," Feb. 1995.
10. *The Week in Review,* CNN, June 27, 1993.
11. *This Week with David Brinkley,* ABC, Aug. 8, 1993.

Appendix: More Things Government Does Right
1. John Carey, "Why Business Doesn't Back the GOP Backlash on the Ozone," *Business Week,* July 24, 1995.
2. As quoted by Daniel Greenberg, "House of Ignorance," *Washington Post,* Oct. 27, 1995.
3. The White House, Briefing Papers on Select Administration Policies, prepared for the 1995 Southern Economic Conference of the President, Mar. 1995.
4. "Good Numbers Are Worth a Great Deal" (editorial), *Business Week,* Aug. 21, 1995.
5. The People Helper, "Cutbacks to CPSC Threaten Us All," *Times-Picayune* (New Orleans), Apr. 28, 1995.

6. Nancy Steorts, "Commission Shows How to Protect Consumers While Respecting Industry," *Washington Times,* May 27, 1995.

7. Wayne D. Rasmussen, *Taking the University to the People* (Ames: Iowa State Univ. Press, 1989), p. 1.

8. Adam Clymer, "GOP Revises a Budget Rule to Help Banks," *New York Times,* Aug. 20, 1995.

9. Jerome Supple, speech to the American Council on Education, San Francisco, CA, Feb. 14, 1995.

10. Department of Education, Direct Loans Fact Sheet, 1995.

11. Ibid.

12. Bob Shireman, "Self-serving Loan Program," *Washington Post,* Aug. 23, 1995.

13. The White House, Briefing Papers on Select Administration Policies, prepared for the 1995 Southern Economic Conference of the President, Mar. 1995.

14. "Family Leave Act Is a Labor Day Success Story" (editorial), *Denver Post,* July 4, 1995.

15. Ibid.

16. J. Linn Allen, "FHA Is at a Crossroads," *Chicago Tribune,* Sept. 17, 1995.

17. Ibid.

18. Ibid.

19. Tony Monroe, "Fat City Is Near For Fans of Tell-All Food Labeling," *Washington Times,* May 3, 1994.

20. Ibid.

21. Veterans Administration, *History of the G.I. Bill,* 1994.

22. Ibid.

23. Jessica Matthews, "Look Before You Lop," *Washington Post,* Mar. 27, 1995.

24. Nicholas Wade, "Rapid Gains Are Reported in Genome," *New York Times,* Sept. 28, 1995.

25. Robert S. Boyd, "DNA Research Project Shows Great Promise: Genetic Code Is Program Target," *Phoenix Gazette,* Sept. 22, 1995.

26. "Crippling American Science" (editorial), *New York Times,* May 23, 1995.

27. Janet Ward, "One Hundred Years of Public Works," *American City and County,* Sept. 1994.

28. Ibid.

29. Joseph P. Kennedy II, testimony before House Committee on Economic and Educational Opportunities, subcommittee on Early Childhood, Youth, and Families, June 28, 1995.

30. Peter T. Kilborn, "Saving Money or Saving Lives: A Bill to Reduce Regulations Alarms Safety Experts," *New York Times,* Sept. 19, 1995.

31. Ibid.

32. Ibid.

33. B. Drummond Ayres, Jr., "Law to Ease Voter Registration Has Added 5 Million to the Rolls," *New York Times,* Sept. 3, 1995.

34. Ibid.

35. Brian Mooar and Bill Miller, "N.C. Officer Arrested Agent's Killer Hours Earlier," *Washington Post,* June 2, 1995.

36. Christina Kent, "On the Block for a Change: National Health Service Corps," *Medical News,* June 19, 1995.

37. Bob Mercer, "South Dakota Wants a Piece of the Rock," *Washington Post,* July 4, 1995.

38. Kathy Sawyer, "Increasing the Accuracies of Foretelling Hurricanes' Deadly Turns," *Washington Post,* July 31, 1995.

39. President William J. Clinton, speech at second anniversary of National Performance Review, Washington, D.C., Sept. 7, 1995.

40. "Peace Corps Nominee to Seek More Volunteers," AP story in *Rocky Mountain News,* July 22, 1995.

41. Department of Labor, *Reemployment Services: A Review of Their Effectiveness,* Apr. 1994.

42. Center on Hunger, Poverty, and Nutrition Policy, Tufts Univ. School of Nutrition, *The Link Between Nutrition and Cognitive Development in Children,* 1995.

43. A. F. Meyers et al., "School Breakfast Program and School Performance," *American Journal of Diseases of Children,* Oct. 1993.

44. The White House, Briefing Papers on Select Administration Policies, prepared for the 1995 Southern Economic Conference, Mar. 1995.

45. Peter T. Kilborn, "Jobs for Elderly Poor Are Targeted for Cuts," *New York Times,* Sept. 15, 1995.

46. Ibid.

47. Jennifer Mangan, "Brain Food: Study Suggests Better Grades Earned by Kids Who Watch Educational TV," *Chicago Tribune,* July 20, 1995.

48. "School Readiness: Educational TV Has a Role," *Daily Report Card,* July 19, 1995.

49. Hillary Rodham Clinton, "PBS Provides Refuge From TV Trash," *Buffalo News,* Aug. 13, 1995.

50. Linda Himelstein, "To Scream, Press O," *Business Week,* May 29, 1995.

51. Miles Benson, "Advisors Study Proposals to Privatize Social Security," *Cleveland Plain Dealer,* Sept. 24, 1995.

52. B. Devaney et al., "The Savings in Medicaid Costs for Newborns and Their Mothers from Prenatal Participation in the WIC Program," *Mathematica Policy Research,* Oct. 1990 and Oct. 1991.

53. General Accounting Office, *Early Intervention: Federal Investments Like WIC Can Produce Saving,* Apr. 1992.

PLEASE CREDIT ANY QUOTES OR EXCERPTS FROM
THIS MBC TELEVISION PROGRAM TO
MBC NEWS' *PRESS THE MEAT.*

MBC News

PRESS THE MEAT

Sunday, December 10, 1995

GUEST: JAMES CARVILLE
Democratic strategist

Moderator: Tim Rustbelt, MBC News
Panel: George F. Willful, *This Week with
David Wrinkly*
Robert Blovak, *Errors and Blovak*

*The following is a sophomoric spoof, the product of a
few too many drinks on an intercontinental flight.
It's goofy, but it ought to be worth a few chuckles.*

MR. RUSTBELT: Welcome again to *Press the Meat*. Our issue this Sunday morning: the desperate ideological battle for the heart and soul of this nation.

Our guest this morning was supposed to be Dick Morris, President Clinton's most trusted adviser. But Mr. Morris was called off to Camp David at the last minute, and we needed a fill-in. That's why we settled for this guy. He needs little introduction. He was recently described as "a pathetic and stupid country bumpkin" in *People* magazine and then earned a coveted spot on *Spy* magazine's "Top 100 Most Annoying People, Places, and Things"—right between the Pope and the Wonder-Bra. He is James Carville, the Ragin' Cajun.

Joining me in the questioning this morning is the distinguished commentator George Willful, the thinking person's favorite conservative. And just to provide a diversity of conservative opinion, to his far right we have the nonthinking person's conservative, Robert Blovak, whom most people know as the more offensive one on *Errors and Blovak*.

Mr. Carville, welcome. Good to have you here this morning.

MR. CARVILLE: Thanks. It's an honor to be on your show, Tim.

MR. RUSTBELT: So I understand that you have a new daughter. Probably too early to tell whether she'll be a Democrat or a Republican, but which of her parents does she look more like?

MR. CARVILLE: Well, Tim, people say she looks a little bit more like me, actually. I think—

MR. BLOVAK: Hey, my friend, there's always hope. Didn't Billy Joel's kid start looking more like her mother at some point?

MR. CARVILLE: Joel who?

MR. RUSTBELT: Never mind that, Mr. Carville. Let's talk about changing diapers. My sources tell me that you're a better agent of change in the political system than in the diaper system, if you know what I mean. Is that fair?

MR. CARVILLE: Well, I have to admit—

MR. BLOVAK: I don't care who changes the damn diapers. I just want you to tell me how your man Bill Clinton is going to go in front of the American people, after three years of—

MR. RUSTBELT: Relax, Bob. On this show we're all nice to each other for the first five minutes, remember?

MR. BLOVAK: [unintelligible]

MR. RUSTBELT: I understand that you're also the father of a new book. I hope I get this right: It's called *We're Right and They're Ring-Kissing, Boot-Licking Toadies of Big Business*?

MR. CARVILLE: Actually, no. That was just the working title. My publishers made me change it. When it hits the bookstores it will have the watered-down, fence-sitting, wishy-washy title *We're Right, They're Wrong*.

MR. RUSTBELT: We'll have to break here for a commercial message. Stay tuned. We'll be back with more hardball questions for James Carville in just a minute.

COMMERCIAL MESSAGE: The stream this baby deer drinks from used to be polluted by hundreds of noxious chemicals. That's because this beautiful meadow used to be a strip mine. We at StripCo repaired the ugly scar upon the land and restored the site to its original natural splendor. Why? Because we were forced to. By a federal law. But what really matters is that it's done. So when you hear that our company destroyed this pristine land, remember this: We fixed most of it. StripCo. Doing the Absolute Minimum Required by Law.

MR. RUSTBELT: We're back on *Press the Meat*, talking with James Carville, a last-minute fill-in for the political guru Dick Morris. Mr. Willful, you have a question for our guest.

MR. WILLFUL: Yes, I do. Mr. Carville, I wish to ask you to focus for a moment on the heroic 104th Congress. I think even you would have to acknowledge that when it comes to delivering on promises, the Republicans in both the House and the Senate have been extremely fastidious indeed.

MR. CARVILLE: You're absolutely right. They have been fastidinous, or whatever that word was. They've delivered more than I ever could have imagined. My problem is who they delivered for. These guys—

MR. WILLFUL: I believe you mean "*whom* they delivered for." Or, to be more proper yet, "for whom they delivered."

MR. CARVILLE: You're absolutely right, George. Thank you.

MR. WILLFUL: You're quite welcome.

MR. CARVILLE: So my problem is for whom they delivered. These guys delivered for every special-interest group who ever wrote them a check. They delivered for the pollution lobby. They delivered for Rupert Murdoch. He got a $63 million tax break and will probably get a killer telecommunications bill worth much more than that. At a time when we've got the richest rich people in the industrialized world and damn near the poorest poor kids, they delivered on making the kids poorer and the rich richer. Ain't no doubt about that. They delivered big-time. It was FedEx next-business-morning-overnight service.

MR. RUSTBELT: Uh, Mr. Carville, maybe we should keep FedEx and Rupert Murdoch out of this. The network boys are a little sensitive about spiked language and lawsuits these days, if you know what I mean.

MR. BLOVAK: I can't believe this. You're worried about lawsuits? What about this man's outrageous display of class warfare?

MR. CARVILLE: I guess you've got to call something what it is. If we have some of the poorest poor children in the industrialized world and we're going to cut infant nutrition programs, Head Start, food stamps, school lunches, college loans and grants, and yet at the same time we're going to cut the capital-gains tax, with most of the benefits going to people in my tax bracket, we do have a class war on our hands. No question about it. Let's just call a spade a spade.

MR. RUSTBELT: Mr. Carville, you don't mean to suggest that the Democrats don't deliver for their contributors. The Democrats are subject to the same special-interest pressures, are they not?

MR. CARVILLE: I'm not stupid enough to sit here and tell you that Democrats have never cozied up to a special interest. But you've got to know the difference between speeding and highway robbery. Never in my time have I seen what we're seeing now: lobbyists sitting in Representative Tom De Lay's office, cranking out talking points and amendments. Lobbyists calling federal agencies and announcing themselves as representing congressional committees. It's one thing to sit and listen and meet with people, and it's another to have them in your office writing your legislation!

Mr. Rustbelt: It's getting a bit hot around here. Let's have a word from our sponsor. We'll be right back.

COMMERCIAL MESSAGE: Here at the Major Motors plant in Smithville, Michigan, we know that someday one of these air bags just might save your life. That's why airbags are a standard safety feature in all our new models. Also, they're required. By a federal regulation. A regulation that we fought like dogs to avert. But when we lost, we turned on a dime and immediately started featuring air bags in our commercials. Major Motors. We Roll with the Punches.

Mr. Rustbelt: We're back on *Press the Meat* with James Carville. In the last election, Mr. Carville, you came up with three buzz phrases to keep you and your candidate focused. The first of those phrases, "The economy, stupid," has now been quoted more than two thousand times in the press. What are the three phrases that are going to do it for you this time around?

Mr. Carville: Funny you should ask that, Tim. I suppose now's as good a time as any to roll them out.

[Mr. Carville performs drumroll on Mr. Blovak's head. Mr. Willful gasps.]

Mr. Blovak: Hey, cut that out!

Mr. Willful: Gasp!

Mr. Carville: And here they are, ladies and gentlemen. Just what you've been waiting for. The mantra for '96:

> Number one: It's paychecks, stupid
> Number two: Daddies matter—big-time
> Number three: Don't turn back the clock

Let me explain what I mean here. "It's paychecks, stupid" means we've got to keep working toward making our economy perform for most people, not just for the folks at the top. While we've certainly had an exceedingly strong economy under this President, the effects of that strength have yet to be felt not only by those at the bottom of the economy but also by those in the middle. Right now, we have by far the biggest gap between haves and have-nots in the entire industrialized world. Republicans say that's a sign of a healthy capitalistic society—a cause for celebration. I happen to disagree.

By "Daddies matter" I mean that Senator Moynihan was right a long time ago: A big problem that we face in this country is the breakup of the family. I'm not just talking about welfare families. In every part of America we're seeing an increasing number of children that are growing up in single-parent households. And all of the available data and research indicate that this is causing an enormous social and economic crisis. So this is clearly something else we have to hit hard.

By "Don't turn back the clock" I mean that we have made some remarkable progress in this country. We've cut in half the rate of poverty among the elderly. We've increased the number of high school graduates. We can drink our water and breathe our air again. This is no time to go backward. Our poor children ranked sixteenth of eighteen industrialized nations in terms of child poverty. We don't need to turn the clock back to where we're eighteenth. It's bad enough that we're sixteenth.

MR. BLOVAK: There he goes again! How can you two let him get away with this? He's walking all over you. What kind of talk show is this, anyway?

MR. CARVILLE: Actually, Mr. Blovak, it's not a talk show. It's just a corny device in my book. I guess I forgot to tell you.

MR. BLOVAK: Oh.

MR. WILLFUL: You didn't tell me, either. I feel so used! So victimized!

MR. BLOVAK: Quit your blubbering, Willful. We conservatives do not believe in victimization, remember?

MR. WILLFUL: You're quite right, Mr. Blovak. I lost my head for a moment. Do forgive me.

MR. RUSTBELT: Well, that's about all the time we have this week. Mr. Carville, we want to thank you for appearing on *Press the Meat*. It was so good of you to fill in on such short notice. And good luck in November.

MR. CARVILLE: Thanks. Thanks for having me.

MR. RUSTBELT: That's all for this week's edition of *Press the Meat*. Join us next Sunday for a discussion of the wing nuts in the Republican Party. Our guest: Fat Pukanan, the Presidential candidate who was intolerant and xenophobic before intolerance and xenophobia were cool.

JAMES CARVILLE, cofounder of the political consulting firm Carville & Begala, is an adviser to President Bill Clinton. He is also coauthor, with his wife, Mary Matalin, of *All's Fair: Love, War, and Running for President*; the couple live with their daughter, Matty, in Maurertown, Virginia. Carville is a regular guest on network television and radio, including Tony Kornheiser's program, where he offers his football picks against the point spread.

ABOUT THE TYPE

This book was set in Bembo, a typeface based on an old-style Roman face that was used for Cardinal Bembo's tract *De Aetna* in 1495. Bembo was cut by Francisco Griffo in the early sixteenth century. The Lanston Monotype Machine Company of Philadelphia brought the well-proportioned letter forms of Bembo to the United States in the 1930s.